ALSO BY STEDMAN GRAHAM

Teens Can Make It Happen

You Can Make It Happen

MOVE
WITHOUT THE
BALL

• •

PUT YOUR SKILLS AND YOUR MAGIC
TO WORK FOR YOU!

STEDMAN
GRAHAM

A FIRESIDE BOOK
Published by Simon & Schuster
New York London Toronto Sydney

FIRESIDE
Rockefeller Center
1230 Avenue of the Americas
New York, NY 10020

For information regarding special discounts for bulk purchases,
please contact Simon & Schuster Special Sales at 1–800–456–6798
or business@simonandschuster.com

Designed by Helene Berinsky

Manufactured in the United States of America

10   9   8   7   6   5   4   3   2   1

Library of Congress Cataloging–in–Publication Data is available.

ISBN 0–7432–3440–5

CONTENTS

ACKNOWLEDGMENTS

In step seven in the book *You Can Make It Happen*™, a nine-step plan for success, I talk about "Building Your Dream Team." I want to thank the original *Move Without the Ball*™ dream team for helping to make this project the great one that it is. Our Founding Member Dream Team is comprised of:

Maya Angelou
Bob Brown, B&C Associates, Inc.
Robert Johnson, BET Holdings, Inc.
Coker College
Crest Communications
Mark Victor Hansen
Patricia J. Hansen
Tim Bennett, Harpo Productions, Inc.
Dianne Atkinson Hudson
Michael W. Hudson
Danny C. Lawson
Mark Gambill, Manpower
Karen Neuburger
Paul Adams, Providence St. Mel High School

I want to especially thank the Coker College team: Dr. B. James Dawson, president; Dr. Ronald L. Carter, provost and dean of the faculty; and Dr. James W. Lemke, director of the Center for Research, Leadership, and Community Development. They have been pivotal in the development of a program beyond this book. Given their ongoing commitment to community building and the development of a highly regarded college, it gives me great pleasure to be a part of the distinguished faculty there.

I want to thank Tom Hanlon, who assisted in researching, writing, and organizing this book. He is very talented.

I also want to thank Wendy Graham for her attention to detail, her conceptualization, and the energy she has given to this project. She is an ambassador in making projects happen.

I want to thank Jan Miller, my literary agent, for her unwavering support.

I want to thank the team at Simon & Schuster, especially Carolyn Reidy, president and publisher, and Dominick Anfuso, editorial director. They have believed in me throughout the years, and supported the writing and development of nearly all of my books and projects.

Most important, I dedicate this book to the many teens who I hope will benefit from it and will use these examples and stories as a metaphor for looking at one's whole life. It is important to take examples from all walks of life and all kinds of people. I hope this book will serve as a catalyst and an inspiration to teach young people to Move Without the Ball.

THE YARMO GREEN STORY

Yarmo Green was a young man with high hopes and dreams in 1994.

He was an All–Public League running back in football at Mather High School in Chicago. He had hopes of playing football for Notre Dame, and aspirations for a career in the National Football League.

Neither of those dreams came close to happening, because he made some decisions that landed him in prison. Now his hope is to be paroled when he first becomes eligible, which will be in 2014—when he will be thirty–seven years old. Even if he's paroled then, he will have spent more than half his life in prison.

Yarmo is serving a forty–year sentence for attempted murder, having been convicted of nearly bludgeoning a rival gang member to death.

In an article published on June 12, 2001, in the *Chicago Sun-Times*, writer Taylor Bell quotes Green as saying, "If I had the opportunity to give some advice to a kid from my old neighborhood, I would tell him the real deal about the streets. The truth is, taking of young lives is senseless, and fast times and fast money are dangerous. Kids are easily excited by the lifestyle of a drug dealer. I would do my best to dispel this myth and assure them that they are loved more by their parents and siblings than by those who might befriend them in the street."

Green had lived in a neighborhood where gang activity was

Yarmo Green

rampant. Like many in his situation, he chose to be part of a gang partly out of survival. Other factors no doubt weighed in on his choice.

The choice has cost him a lot of years and will cost him many more.

To Yarmo's credit, he has earned his general equivalency diploma (GED) in prison. He wants to further his education and is interested in business management. "Earning my GED was a challenge for me, a bigger challenge than playing football, because I was developing my intellect rather than using my physical and athletic capabilities," he says in the *Sun-Times* article. "It was an individual accomplishment rather than a team effort. . . . I've learned that I can succeed in life as well. I don't need the neighborhood, I don't need to live that lifestyle anymore. I'm moving forward, not backward."

He plays basketball, tries to keep physically active. He believes that life still has much to offer and is focused on moving forward toward a better life once he is released, a very different life from the one he knew.

Yarmo Green has a long way to go, and though his hopes and dreams have changed, he still has hope. "It's not over for me," he says. "It's the fourth quarter and I'm down a lot of years. . . . Don't give up on me because I'm not giving up on myself. I'm still running on hope."

WHAT "MOVE WITHOUT THE BALL" MEANS

Yarmo Green was a tremendous prep athlete with a world of potential. He knew exactly how to move *with* the ball, and he moved with it extremely well.

It was in moving *without* the ball that he stumbled and fell.

What do I mean by moving without the ball? Let me begin my explanation by telling you what got *me* moving without the ball.

. . . .

My focus, as with many young people, was to be a professional athlete. Looking back on that goal, I realize that I really didn't know how to accomplish that or to come close to reaching my full potential as an athlete, let alone as a person.

I was a star athlete in Whitesboro, New Jersey. By the time I was a freshman in high school, I started getting recruiting letters from colleges to play basketball for them. Those letters began piling up as I continued to excel. By my junior and senior years, those letters were arriving almost daily. I had earned All-State honors, and I had colleges all across the country telling me that I should come play for them. My head was spinning as I sifted through all the offers.

One day I was at Mr. T. A.'s, a soda shop and game arcade where high school kids hung out. T. A. Richardson was one of the few African-American men in town who owned his own business, and as such he was somebody a lot of people looked up to, myself included. I mentioned to Mr. T. A. that I was getting all these recruiting letters and was in the midst of choosing which college to attend. I expected congratulations and well-wishes, but what I got was a comment that hurt me deeply: "You'll never make it," he said. "You won't graduate or make anything of yourself, because your family is too stupid."

I was the first from my family to go to college. I had always been an average student; I did all right but I never had much confidence in my academic abilities. I focused most of my energy on sports, where I was more sure of myself. I have two brothers, Jimmy and Darry, who are developmentally disabled. I had dreams of making something of myself, of being a basketball star, but here was a role model I looked up to telling me flat out that I didn't have a chance.

Mr. T. A. was someone the whole community looked up to. After I got over the hurt and the disappointment of having him tell me I wasn't going to make it, I got mad. And I promised myself that I was going to get my degree and take it back to Mr. T. A. and show him that I was somebody.

You know what? As hard as those words were for me to hear, they proved invaluable to me. My motivation to succeed, to make something of myself, took on a keener edge than it had before. I didn't like being told that I couldn't do something, and I wanted to prove Mr. T. A. wrong. His comments made me think outside my own box, which at that time was comprised entirely of my athletic success. This guy was saying I couldn't cut it *academically*. He offered me a challenge, and I responded.

Four years later, after attaining my college degree from Hardin-Simmons University in Abilene, Texas, I walked back into Mr. T. A.'s and told him the news. He was happy for me and pleased that I had gotten my degree. He didn't realize what a driving force he had been behind my growth as a student. Mr. T. A.'s comments helped me expand my vision of myself, painful as the comments were and uncertain as I was of myself beyond my abilities as an athlete.

Actually, Mr. T. A. was half right. I didn't make my original dream of playing in the National Basketball Association (NBA). I played college ball, and I played ball in Europe after college. But, thanks in part to Mr. T. A's comments, I expanded my vision. I realized there was more to life than basketball. I realized I could make something of myself *beyond* sports.

Mr. T. A. sounded my wake-up call to move without the ball, and I'm grateful for that.

Now I'm trying to do the same for you.

. . . .

I now realize that education is important, but to be truly successful I had to make education relevant to my life. In school I learned to memorize, take tests, and get labeled by grades, and two weeks later I probably forgot most of the information. I fell into a routine of doing the same thing over and over every day, and I began to wonder if I did the same thing tomorrow that I did today, where was I going?

In my younger years I never knew how to think, how to create opportunities, how to reinvent myself, because I allowed myself to be programmed by other people who defined my potential for me based on my race, my background, my class, and also my label as a basketball player. I was focused on validating myself through sports. I'd prove how good a person I was because I could play basketball well.

I didn't realize that I was limiting myself when I thought of myself only as a basketball player. My vision for myself was no bigger than my present circumstances. Your vision has to become bigger, or you just stay in the same place your whole life.

So when we talk about moving without the ball we are talking about thinking, about creating a vision for yourself. We all have twenty-four hours in one day. The question becomes what are we going to do with the twenty-four hours that we are given, which cannot be stored away, regardless of who we are. How do we create the life we want and perform at the levels we want, based on our gifts and talents?

Move Without the Ball teaches process. As I lecture around the country in all types of settings—to young people, for organizations, at colleges and universities, and to corporate America—I find that we are missing the ability to process. We know we want the sizzle, we know we want to win and feel good about the victory or rewards or the title. We want the cars, the money, the houses, and the fame, but what no one teaches us, in school or out, is the *process* for reaching our dreams and goals. We need to know how to handle the in-between stuff, the part no one gives us credit for; but unless we go through the process, reaching each goal one step at a time, we cannot realize our dreams.

As a former high school athlete, as a college player, as a European pro leaguer, I look back and I realize the value sports played in my life. I learned about teamwork, dedication, and the value of never quitting. I learned how the game itself (and how the game of life) can change. I learned the realities of having to listen to someone and also having to do something when I didn't want to. These are all lessons you can apply not just to sports but to your job, or a particular project, with your family, and to your life, in general. It is about doing the best you can and understanding the process of moving without the ball.

DEFINING "MOVE WITHOUT THE BALL"

I'm sure you've seen images on TV of lions chasing gazelles on the African plains. The lions have one thing on their minds: dinner. The gazelles, likewise, have one thing on their minds: survival. If a gazelle walks, or ambles about aimlessly, it becomes dinner. If it runs with purpose and determination, calling on all its abilities to elude the lions, it lives another day.

When you learn to live your life with purpose and determination, and call on your abilities to excel in whatever you pursue, you will be successful. You will be moving without the ball.

When you move well without the ball, these things happen:

- You come closer to reaching your full potential in life, both in and out of sports.

- You move toward your goals; you pursue life with a purpose and a passion.
- You understand that your life is filled with choices, and those choices have consequences, and you steer toward the choices that will help you reach your potential and your dreams and goals.
- You no longer shy away from challenges; you rise up to meet them head-on.
- You build life skills that will serve you well now and in the future.
- You open up numerous opportunities for yourself to achieve what you want to achieve and to live a full and satisfying life.

Move without the ball, then, is an approach to life that you can take, and benefit from, no matter who you are and what your present circumstances are. Yarmo Green is moving without the ball right now, even though he's in prison. He's preparing himself for life after prison, and he's doing what he can to get all he can out of life while he's in prison, though he's under obvious constraints and restrictions.

Unless you're in prison as well, you're free to move without the ball and experience more immediate gratification from doing so. But just as momentum is crucial in sports, so it is in life. You have to keep the momentum going. You don't begin to move and then put your life on cruise control and expect it all to work out. You keep moving in the direction you want your life to take, you keep applying your energy to that movement.

THE NEED TO MOVE WITHOUT THE BALL

Move without the ball is an approach to life that is embraced by all successful people—athletes, musicians, scientists, doctors, lawyers, businesspeople, entrepreneurs, and on and on.

They're successful because they're moving without the ball.

Think about it in these terms: let's say you're playing basketball and you're standing still while you don't have the ball, not moving or trying to get open. What happens? *Nothing* happens—except that the game will literally pass you by. You don't help your team, you don't enjoy the game, and you get nothing out of your skills.

If you *do* move without the ball, you are helping your team. You get open, you receive a pass, and you go in to score, or maybe you pass to a teammate cutting to the basket. Movement makes it happen in basketball.

It makes it happen in life, too. If you're coasting in school, not studying, getting poor grades, making no plans for the future, just goofing off (or, worse, getting in trouble with the law), you're wasting your talent, your time, your potential. And life will pass you by. The value you give yourself is the value the world gives you.

To move without the ball in life means to prepare yourself, to apply yourself, to create goals for yourself that are in line with your talents and desires, and to aggressively and wisely pursue your goals.

Are you ready to move without the ball?

GET READY TO MOVE!

Derron is a prep basketball player who believes he can get an athletic scholarship to college.

Lisa is a prep softball player who rarely plays in her team's games, but she loves the sport and the experience.

Maria is in the National Honor Society and has designs on getting a master's degree in engineering.

Nathan is sliding by in school with no real plans for the future.

All four of them need to focus on moving without the ball. As do you. It doesn't matter if you're a student–athlete or a student who doesn't participate in sports. It doesn't matter if you're struggling or doing well in sports or school or other pursuits. You still need to learn how to move without the ball.

Now, I can't make your dreams come true. I have no magic wand, no crystal ball, no foreknowledge of what the future holds for you.

But I have a wealth of experience that relates directly to your life, and where I took the long way around, I can show you a short-cut. Where I struggled, I can guide you in achieving your goals with less struggle. Where I hesitated for a while to expand my horizons, I can help you expand yours by showing you how to translate your athletic or scholastic achievements to a success that is not only beyond sports and school but probably, at this moment, beyond your wildest imagination.

That's part of what this book is about: imagination. I'm not talking about lofty dreams that have no connection to the real world. I'm talking about imagining a great and fulfilling life for yourself—and then understanding the practical steps to achieving what you imagine.

This book is all about you shaping your goals and reaching them: your goals as a student, as an athlete, as a person.

It's all about you reaching your full potential in all areas of your life—in sports and beyond sports.

It's all about you, regardless of who you are or what your aspirations are.

A NOTE ON TERMINOLOGY

I've just said this book is for all students, whether they are athletes or not. This is very true. For that matter, it is equally applicable to students in middle school, junior high, high school, and college—not to mention people who are no longer in school.

For the sake of consistency, I'm going to generally use sports examples and speak to you as if you are a student–athlete. I'm going to use sports as a metaphor for life. Even if you're not in sports, the same principles apply to your life. Those principles will help you achieve your potential in any field or endeavor.

If you aren't an athlete, allow your mind to grasp the concepts of athletic success, and apply those concepts to your own pursuits.

Okay? Let's move on to what you'll get out of this book.

WHAT YOU'LL LEARN FROM THIS BOOK

Through this book, you will

- identify and explore *all* your talents—athletic, academic, and otherwise—and learn how to get the most out of them;
- view success as going beyond the confines of sports;

- begin to shape visions and goals for yourself beyond sports;
- determine what life skills are most important and how to build them;
- learn how to identify and overcome challenges;
- examine the keys to enhancing your performance, and your life, through health and fitness;
- realize that you really have much greater control of your destiny than you probably imagine.

You'll learn from athletes who have experienced great success both in sports and beyond. You'll get an inside glimpse into their success and how they achieved it. These athletes include Vince Carter, Mia Hamm, Hank Aaron, Julius Erving, Serena Williams, Jerry Rice, Dave Winfield, and Magic Johnson. You'll learn from numerous other athletes as well.

Finally, you'll learn how to make success a habit, how to keep on moving with and without the ball.

This book can change your life—if you're ready for change.

Are you ready to move?

1

EXCEL IN SPORTS

VINCE CARTER: MAN OF MANY NAMES, SINGULAR SKILL

His full name is Vincent Lamar Carter, but he goes by various nick-names: Vinsanity, InVINCEible, Air Canada, Elevator Man, and others. People who have seen Carter play basketball strive to come up with superlative nicknames to match the skills of the six–foot–six swingman, who was the fifth pick in the 1998 NBA draft. Carter led the North Carolina Tar Heels to an 83–22 record and two Final Fours in his three years there and now stars for the Toronto Raptors in the NBA.

Carter has lived up to his nicknames. For a few career highlights, see the box below.

Vince Carter NBA Highlights

Points per game, career:	24.1
Points per game, play-offs:	25.7
Career high, game:	51 points
Rebounds per game, career:	5.5
Rebounds per game, play-offs:	6.4
Assists per game, career:	3.7
Assists per game, play-offs:	5.0

Toronto Raptors' Vince Carter—not one-dimensional in his game or in his life.

Carter was the overwhelming choice for Rookie of the Year for the 1998–99 season, receiving 96 percent of the votes. He represented the United States at the 2000 Olympics in Sydney, leading the team in scoring at 14.8 points per game and helping the United States win the gold medal.

As Carter's statistics show, he is far from one-dimensional in his game. The same goes for his life outside of basketball. He established the Embassy of Hope Foundation to support children's causes, initiated "Vince's Hoop Group," a program that recognizes students' achievements at a school in Toronto, and was named a Goodwill Ambassador by Big Brothers Big Sisters of America.

The Embassy of Hope generates hundreds of thousands of dollars each year for Toronto children's charities. Carter says he decided to establish the Embassy of Hope Foundation to help make a difference by encouraging young people to believe in their dreams.

Carter followed his own dream to NBA stardom, but not at the neglect of his college education. Though he left North Carolina after his junior year to join the NBA, he returned to North Carolina to finish college and earn his bachelor's degree.

He returned to school in part because he knew the eyes of lots of schoolkids were on him. He is used to showing young athletes how to move with the ball; he does that every game he plays in the NBA. By returning to college to earn his bachelor's degree, he showed young players how to move without the ball as well.

DON'T JUST *TALK* A GREAT GAME . . .

You can learn to move without the ball, just as Vince Carter did. You can also learn to move *with* the ball. But it will take more than dreaming about success.

This world is filled with dreamers. Don't get me wrong, dreaming is an essential part of success. But the problem with most people is they don't get beyond the dreaming. What separates successful people from the crowd is they use their dreams to fuel their actions.

They don't just dare to dream; they dare to *act*.

It costs you nothing to sit around and daydream about how great life would be if you were an NBA superstar, or if you were the next great running back in the NFL, or if you took the pro tennis circuit by storm and made Serena and Venus Williams yesterday's news.

But it costs you plenty to act upon any of those dreams. It costs you hours and seasons and years of hard work. It costs you time and money and energy. It costs you hobbies and time vegging out and time just hanging with your friends.

It costs you your very dream itself, because it forces you to either achieve it or give it up, to pursue it or call it quits. No longer can you hide behind statements like "Well, I could have done this or achieved that if I'd really tried," or "I should've done it this way; then I'd have been a superstar," or "I would've been great if only the breaks hadn't gone against me."

Could have, should have, would have.

They get you nowhere.

True superstars don't have time for could have, should have, would have. They have no time for excuses, for whining, for complaining. They're too focused on doing all they can to be the best they can be in their sport.

That's what this chapter is about. You won't become a superstar, necessarily, by following the steps in this chapter. But you *will* take great strides toward realizing your full potential in sports.

That's all you can expect of yourself: to reach your full potential. That much is in your control. Whether you become a superstar is *not* in your control, because that involves stacking your abilities and performance level against others, and you can't control how good other athletes are.

So focus on reaching your full potential and let the chips fall where they may. Just as studies have shown that we use only a small percent of our brain capacity, I think it's also true that most of us don't come near to reaching our full athletic potential. If you come close to reaching yours, then you will make significant improvements in your game and get more enjoyment and mileage out of your athletic career.

What does it take to excel in sports? I think you have to do the following:

1. Know your talent.
2. Understand yourself and your role on the team.

3. Form a vision for yourself and set goals to make that vision happen.
4. Work hard in practice and in training.
5. Have a positive attitude.
6. Communicate and relate appropriately with coaches and teammates.
7. Be confident in your abilities.
8. Be durable and strong in overcoming setbacks.
9. Be hungry for growth and improvement.
10. Be smart.

Let's explore each point. As you read, consider where you stand and how you might improve in each area.

Know Your Talent

There are three mistakes to avoid here:

- You overestimate your talent.
- You underestimate your talent.
- You don't know your strengths and weaknesses as an athlete.

Players who overestimate their talent often coast, partly because they think they're so good they don't need to work hard. They also tend to be selfish, because they think they can "turn it on" and "rescue" their team whenever the game's on the line. They like recognition and attention and do what they can to earn it. These players often *are* talented, but not nearly as talented as they think. They end up hurting their teams because of their selfish play and their lackadaisical attitudes, and they don't reach their full potential, because they don't realize they have to *work* to do so.

Players who underestimate their talent hurt their teams in a different way: they don't contribute in ways that they can. They hold back because they're not confident in their abilities. They make it easy for the defenders to guard them because they don't know the talent they have and don't know how to use it. They don't reach

Dikembe Mutombo—back in his playing days for Georgetown.

their full potential either, just as a driver who drives with one foot on the brake will never reach full speed. These players are their own worst enemy.

Many players don't really know their own strengths and weaknesses. It's difficult to reach your full potential if you aren't aware of what you bring to the game, of how you can help your team, of what you need to work on to improve.

Many players who have excelled in the pros have done so by specializing. In the NBA there are defensive specialists such as Dikembe Mutombo, who isn't a big scorer but who consistently shuts down opposing centers. There are rebounding specialists such as Detroit's Ben Wallace and Golden State's Danny Fortson. There are scoring specialists such as Detroit's Corliss Williamson and Dallas's Nick Van Exel, who come off the bench to provide offensive spark. In baseball there are left-handed relief pitchers who make careers out of pitching to one or two left-handed hitters every other game. There are pinch-hitting specialists and defensive replacements, guys who are swift and graceful and superb fielders but who can't hit well.

The point is this: all those players know their talent, know what they can do for their team, and they hone their skills and provide what their team needs. They get everything out of their talent—and that's all their coaches and managers can ask.

Are there more talented all-around players than the ones I mentioned? Absolutely. And they're sitting at home, watching these players perform on TV, because the ones still performing are experts at knowing their value to a team and how to get the most out of their talent.

As you consider your talents, think about what has worked for you in the past, about the areas or skills you are most confident in, where you feel most capable. Think about some of your greatest athletic achievements and how you achieved them.

Charles Barkley: Know Your Talents Expand *Beyond* Sports

Charles Barkley is a former NBA star who is not shy with his opinions. Perhaps surprising to those who followed his career, Barkley is *not* high on sports, at least not in the way so many African–American teens get it in their heads, that if they can't make it as a professional athlete, then they can't make it at all. Such sentiment infuriates Barkley.

No matter what color you are, your value as a person and your potential in life expand far beyond sports. Remember that.

Charles Barkley: Know who you are beyond sports.

Understand Yourself and Your Role on the Team

Kerry Ligtenberg pitched for baseball's Atlanta Braves in the late 1990s and the early part of this decade. For a few seasons he was asked to be their closer—the pitcher who came in and shut the door at the end of the game, saving the game for his team. He performed in this role quite effectively.

Then John Smoltz took over the closing role for the Braves, and Ligtenberg was moved to setup man. He was asked to hold the score, to pitch an inning or so in the late innings and hand the ball off to Smoltz with the lead intact as Smoltz performed the more glamorous role of closing the game. Ligtenberg was an exceptional setup man. Though his role changed, he understood what he was being asked to do and went out and did his job, helping his team win. Though he rarely received the headlines, he was one of the key reasons that the Braves were so successful in the 1990s and in the early part of this decade.

• • • • • • • •

If I were a basketball coach and I were asked if I wanted a group of talented prima donnas or a group of moderately skilled players who worked hard and understood the team concept and their roles on the team, I'd say you keep the prima donnas and give me the moderately skilled role-players. In fact, I'd say let's schedule the team of prima donnas and show them what a team sport is all about.

Coaches love players who understand their roles, because that understanding—and the fulfillment of those roles—helps the team accomplish its goals. To stay with basketball for a moment, there are team leaders and go-to guys; there are defensive and rebounding specialists; there are three-point shooters and playmakers; there are guys who are in there to take a charge and dive for loose balls and do the things that don't show up in the box score; there are even free-throw shooting specialists who are in at the end of close games to handle the ball and preserve the lead at the foul line.

There are roles for athletes in every sport. When you understand your strengths and weaknesses and how you fit into the team plan, you can focus on fulfilling your role. Yours might be a starring role or a supporting role; that doesn't matter. What does matter is that you understand the role and focus all your attention on fulfilling it.

> Talk to your coach if you are at all unclear about your role. Ask also about ways to excel in this role. Your coach is in the best position to help you know what to work on to improve your abilities in your role.

Form a Vision for Yourself and Set Goals to Make that Vision Happen

Dan Gable was first a wrestler, and later a coach, with great vision. He set his goals very high and then he went out and, guided by his vision, achieved his goals. As a wrestler, he suffered only one loss (in his final NCAA match of his career), and he won a gold medal in the Olympics. As a coach, Gable guided his Iowa Hawkeyes to 15 NCAA team championships, coaching 45 individual NCAA champions and 152 All-Americans along the way.

Great athletes have clear visions. They know where they want to go and how they plan to get there. That vision is invaluable as they go through the work and the pain, the challenges and the setbacks, the ups and downs of a long season or career. That vision is their one constant, the one thing that remains unchanged. And that vision can often make the difference between achieving significant goals and falling short.

To form a vision, you have to know your strengths and capabilities. You have to know yourself, your dreams and desires, and how hard you're willing to work. You have to have courage and constantly ask yourself what is possible. And you have to be willing to challenge yourself day in and day out.

Your vision is your ultimate destination, what you're aiming for. As your talents grow, as you gain more experience and understanding about yourself, your vision can grow.

Your goals, on the other hand, are the checkpoints along the way to realizing your vision. If your vision at sixteen is to be a future Olympic 100-meter champion, certainly a few of your goals would be to win your conference 100 meters, probably to win the state championship, to earn a track scholarship to a major track school, and to improve your personal best each year.

Your goals let you know how you're doing in your attempt to realize your vision. Make sure your goals are realistic and challenging. If they're *too* challenging and unrealistic—if the sixteen-year-old track star determines he's going to win Olympic gold when he's sixteen—then the goals are pointless and don't help the athlete. If the goal is too easy—if the track star simply wants to beat his competition in his area, and he's already proven he's far superior to them—that doesn't help the athlete either. Put your goals out there, but set goals that can be realistically achieved through consistent hard work, focus, and steady improvement.

> Form your vision for yourself as an athlete around the skills you have. Where do you most excel, and why? Don't be afraid to take a cold, hard look at yourself—and don't be afraid to dream. Ground your vision in your own reality of who you are and what you have accomplished so far, and then imagine how you can expand that reality based on your own talents and desires. Dare to dream, then dare to act upon that dream.

Paul Wylie: Forming a New Vision for Himself

Paul Wylie formed a vision for himself as an athlete, and in acting out that vision he won a silver medal in the 1992 Winter Olympics in figure skating. For many years he was one of the world's best skaters, and his abilities took him all over the world, from competition to competition.

When he retired in 1998, he formed another vision for himself—unlike so many athletes who don't prepare themselves for life after sports. Wylie enrolled in Harvard Business School and is now a marketing executive for the Walt Disney Company. He skates now for recreation, content in his transition to life after sports.

Paul Wylie with Nancy Kerrigan

Work Hard in Practice and in Training

Walter Payton, the Hall of Fame running back for the Chicago Bears, was not the biggest running back around, or the fastest. He was simply the best.

Talent? Yes, Walter had talent. But so did a lot of other running backs. What set Walter apart was his determination to be the best, his unbridled passion for the game, and his willingness to work hard. Very hard.

Payton had a hill near his home, a hill with a very steep grade. He would routinely work out on it, chugging up it as hard as he could, then sprinting down it to run up it again. And again. And again.

Teammates and other professional athletes would try to keep up with Payton on his hill. No one could. Many lost their lunch trying to do so. Walter just kept going, driven to be the best, whipping his body into shape so he could not only withstand the punishment doled out by much larger defenders but also dole some of his own out on them. Once a coach caught him doing 525-pound dead lifts on a pulled hamstring. Another time he ran for 125 yards in a game—on a broken toe. Walter wasn't afraid of a little pain, and he knew the meaning of work.

You can be talented and have a vision for yourself, but that won't matter much if you're not willing to work hard. Many gifted athletes are far superior to their competition in middle school and junior

Chicago Bears' running back Walter Payton—one of the hardest-working athletes, and one of the very best.

high, and some of these athletes fall into bad habits, thinking everything will come easy to them throughout their athletic careers.

One of the keys to turning that potential loose is consistent hard work, as defined by 100 percent effort in all practices. The time to coast is when you are a grandparent showing your grandkids your press clippings from yesteryear. The time to devote full effort, if you want to reach your potential, is now.

That means off-season as well as in season. You can't expect to excel if you lose your fitness in the off-season. Great athletes don't turn it on and off when they want to. They keep it turned on. They keep in shape and they keep focused and mentally sharp year-round.

Part of working hard, then, is mental preparation. You of course need to work hard physically, but the superior athletes are just as sharp in the mental aspects of the game as they are in the physical aspects. That means you're on top of game strategy, you know the ins and outs of the game, and you have prepared yourself mentally to perform to the best of your ability. So many athletes have great physical skills but are weak in their mental approach. They don't know how to take advantage of their physical abilities. They freeze; they see themselves through the eyes of the fans or the coach; they hold a debate with themselves on every move they might make—and by the time they make up their minds, the chance to make the move is gone.

True champions are strong both mentally and physically, and that mental and physical preparation is ongoing hard work.

Working hard doesn't mean you're sprinting at all times in practice. It means you're fully tuned in and giving the appropriate effort. It means you're focused on improving every day, and you approach each practice with that in mind. When you bring that focus to your practices, you'll be motivated to work hard.

Have a Positive Attitude

We've all heard of the superstars in pro sports who are described by teammates as "cancers" in the clubhouse or locker room. Some superstars want special treatment from their coaches and the team; they are self-absorbed and care only about their individual statistics and getting lots of media attention. Their egos are too big to fit into the clubhouse or locker room.

Not all superstars have this attitude, of course. In fact, most have very good attitudes, positive and focused on helping their teams win. You have to have your head in every game and every practice; you have to be willing to go the extra mile. You can't shrink in fear of a strong opponent; you have to believe in the strategy your coach has devised and be completely focused on doing your part to make that strategy work.

With a positive attitude, your mind is filled with possibilities and visions of individual improvement and team accomplishment. You are fueled by desire and determination, and you shut out fear and doubt.

With a positive attitude, you are far more likely to reach your full athletic potential. I can guarantee you that the majority of key players on any championship team possess at least one thing in common: a positive attitude. Such an attitude creates a winning environment.

Don't waste time pointing fingers at teammates or coaches for holding you back. One of the biggest things to hold a player back is a negative attitude. Focus on what you can do to improve your own skills and to help your team reach its goals. Check yourself when you begin to make negative statements (either internally or out loud). Change "You should have . . ." or "You didn't . . ." statements into "I can . . ." or "I will . . ." statements.

Communicate and Relate Appropriately with Coaches and Teammates

Players with positive attitudes typically communicate well with teammates and coaches. Communicating with and relating well to teammates and coaches is important to your own development as a player, because a tense environment where there's constant friction between players or between yourself and your coach makes it difficult to focus on improving and getting the most out of your abilities.

Most people think communication is all about *talking*; while your ability to express yourself is certainly important, equally important is your ability to *listen*. If you think you "know" what a teammate or coach is going to say before he or she begins to speak, chances are you're not going to hear that person. Your teammates—and your coaches—deserve your respect, and that means you hear them out. In the case of coaches, that means you not only hear them out but you follow their directions. You can always respectfully discuss, after practice or a game, the directions or strategy, with *respect* being the key issue here.

Good communication also involves how well you communicate with teammates during games. The best teams are like well-oiled machines, with players almost instinctively knowing how teammates are going to act. Much of this game communication is verbal, but more of it is nonverbal—through body language, facial expression, and subtle movements.

Keep the air cleared; be forthright in your comments. Don't hold thoughts and feelings in if you feel strongly about them—but don't try to force your feelings on other people either. Show respect to coaches and teammates as you communicate your feelings and concerns. Understand that other people are going to have other feelings—and in the case of coaches, you have to not only respect their feelings but follow their directions, too. If you and a teammate can't peacefully clear the air by yourselves, take it to your coach.

Be Confident in Your Abilities

Confidence comes from knowing what you can do. It comes from believing that you can do it again, because you've done it in the past. Confident athletes see themselves succeeding before the game occurs or before the big play happens. Because of past success, and because they see themselves succeeding in the present, they *want* the play to come to them. Such desire, when coupled with ability and confidence, is nearly unstoppable.

Confident players aren't afraid to lose or to fail, though they don't envision themselves doing so. Confident athletes know there's a tomorrow and they'll get another chance. A loss or a setback fuels their desire to perform in the clutch, and to succeed, all the more.

Coaches love confident players. One of the greatest frustrations a coach can have is a player who is talented but not confident. A moderately talented player with confidence is often more valuable to his or her team than a very talented player with no confidence.

Understand that *confidence* does not equate with *big ego, trash talk,* or *ball hog.* In my experience, players who talk trash aren't very confident of their skills, so they make up for it by *talking* a big game. Good players just go out and play and let their games talk for themselves. They also step up and perform *within* the team context.

Visualize your success before it happens. See, in your mind's eye, the proper execution of the key skills you need to perform. See yourself executing in clutch situations. Keep external distractions and negative thoughts out. And keep the game in perspective: the world will keep on going whether you win or lose, whether you execute well or not.

Be Durable and Strong in Overcoming Setbacks

I mentioned Walter Payton a few pages back. Walter was an extremely durable football player. He carried the ball 3,838 times, more than any running back in NFL history. He missed one game in thirteen years, an incredible feat in a brutal sport in which injury is commonplace—especially among running backs, who take a beating not only week in and week out but practice in and practice out.

As an athlete, you need to be durable both physically and mentally. As you know, there are plenty of highs and lows in most seasons. You go on a five-game winning streak and you think you'll never be beaten again. You lose three in a row and you privately wonder if you'll ever win again. You encounter personal setbacks as well: injuries, or not playing up to expectations, or being benched in midseason.

The mark of true champions is how they respond to personal and team setbacks. Champions don't lose heart; they don't give in; they toughen themselves and focus on improving their skills and their performance. They look forward, not behind. They live in the present, not the past. They know the tide can turn, things can go their way again. They know the season is long and that true champions outlast the season.

This durability and strength is like a sprinter sprinting *past* the finish line, not slowing down ten meters in front of it. Seasons present numerous challenges both for individual athletes and for teams; those players and teams who can respond best to those challenges—throughout the entire season—emerge, if not on top in the standings, at least knowing they got the most out of their abilities.

GERTRUDE EDERLE:
A TRUE CHAMPION WHO WOULDN'T GIVE UP OR GIVE IN

On November 30, 2003, the world lost a ninety-eight-year-old hero whose historic swim across the English Channel in 1926 was equated by the mayor of New York City, James J. Walker, to the feat of Moses parting the Red Sea. This may sound like hyperbole, but at that time, it was unthinkable that a woman could accomplish this. Over one hundred men had attempted the swim before her, only five made it to shore, and Ederle shattered all their times by over two hours. She

Gertrude Ederle turned setbacks and others' doubts into determination to become the first woman to swim across the English Channel.

also accomplished this in the face of brutal weather conditions, including rain, icy waters, cross winds, and heavy swells. The un-friendly waters were filled with poisonous jellyfish, giant freighters, floating debris, and an occasional shark. She actually had to swim thirty-five miles rather than the twenty-one mile distance because of these torrential conditions. Seventy-five years after making history, Ederle told the Associated Press, "People said women couldn't swim the Channel but I proved they could." Her record stood for twenty-four years for men and thirty-five years for women.

Ederle was never afraid of a challenge and never afraid to fail. She believed in her own abilities, despite the fact that few took her seriously and she was often mocked by other swimmers and by sportswriters. Even after winning three Olympic medals in Paris in 1924—with a knee injury—and setting twenty-nine national and international records by age nineteen, few believed she would be up to the challenge of crossing the Channel. Gertrude Ederle spent a lifetime proving others wrong, just as I was motivated by Mr. T. A's low expectations of me. She said, "When somebody tells me I cannot do something, that's when I do it." Her example inspired both women and men to set high goals for themselves, to focus on success, and to move beyond setbacks. During the 1920s, more than sixty thousand women said they were inspired by Ederle to earn American Red Cross swimming certificates.

At the young age of eight, Ederle's physical and mental drive kicked in after nearly drowning in a pond near her grandmother's house. After she was rescued from the water, she vowed to overcome her fear and learn to swim. We all have fears that can hold us back, some real and some imagined. It's true that sometimes facing them head-on is the best way to overcome them. You've heard the saying, "No risk, no reward." That's not the same as doing something risky just to be part of the crowd or just to test fate. The reward can come in many forms, but do it for yourself, to help you grow as an individual. I call it getting out of your comfort zone and stepping into your outer limits, and I'll talk more about that later.

With risk can come failure, but realize it's just a temporary setback and you can start again with a clean slate. Ederle did. Her first attempt to cross the Channel was a huge disappointment. Just seven miles from victory at the English shore, her coach pulled her out of the water claiming Ederle couldn't continue, despite her protests. The act of touching the swimmer disqualified her immediately. Ederle knew in her heart she could have made it and resolved to attempt the swim again and succeed.

Since a bout with the measles at age five, Ederle had poor hearing, and it worsened considerably after swimming the harsh Channel waters twice. She could not continue swimming professionally, but she continued her passion by teaching swimming to deaf children at the Lexington School for the Deaf in New York. She also became a vaudeville performer, a speaker, a consultant to a dress manufacturer, and she starred in a movie about her life.

She was named by *Sports Illustrated, Sports Illustrated for Women,* and CNN/SI as one of the fifty greatest female athletes of the last century.

> Train your mind to face setbacks as challenges you can defeat. Just as the toughest opponents bring out the best in you, setbacks and challenges should do likewise. The next time you face a setback or challenge, plan specific steps you will take to overcome it.

Be Hungry for Growth and Improvement

Many athletes who have reached the top in professional sports say it's harder to repeat a championship season than it is to put together such a season in the first place. Part of the difficulty in repeating, of course, is the fierce competition for the title, but another factor might be that some of the athletes on the championship team aren't quite as hungry to repeat. After all, they've achieved their primary goal.

To get the most out of your abilities, you've got to *always* be hungry. Your hunger is both for team accomplishments and for individual improvement. When I think of hunger, I think of passion. There are lots of good players out there. Aside from skills, what sets the great players apart from the good? It's their passion and hunger, their willingness to pay the price it takes to become great.

Even the very best professionals can always get better: no one's perfect. And the very best professionals realize that there are tons of talented players eager to take their place—which is what will happen if the best athletes begin to coast a bit, lose the edge off their appetites.

Hunger is what kept Michael Jordan coming back to lead the Chicago Bulls to six NBA championships. Hunger is what keeps Randy Johnson of the Arizona Diamondbacks pitching at his best at thirty-nine years of age. Hunger is what drives Barry Bonds out of bed at 6:00 AM in the off-season to start his daily conditioning regimen.

Hunger is what will spur you to greater and greater levels of play. Hunger is what will drive you to train in the rain and snow because you don't want to lose your edge. Hunger says of even the best performances, "Fine, that was good. But it wasn't *enough*."

Hunger can't be taught; it comes from within. Try to honestly assess your performances and consider where you can improve in the next game. Don't be overly critical of yourself—that is, don't get down on yourself—but plan to minimize your errors and maximize your strengths during the next game. Congratulate yourself on good play, but never be completely satisfied. Look to improve gradually throughout the season, and come back hungry for greater improvement the next season.

Pete Sampras: A Steady Diet of Winning

Some athletes lose their hunger once they reach the top. Not so with Pete Sampras. The tennis great has more Grand Slam titles—fourteen—than any male player in history, and has six year-end No. 1 rankings, again the most ever. He also has more career wins (762) and career earnings ($43 million) than any player in history. Not surprising, in 1997 Sampras was voted the No. 1 player in history by current and past players, journalists, and tournament directors.

Sampras hasn't been idle off the court either. He is a financial stakeholder in the Tennis Channel and in the Pete Sampras Tennis Academy, a training camp for elite young players. He plans to be actively involved in both—and in doing so, the tennis star will be applying what made him successful on the court to his off-the-court ventures.

Be Smart

This final point concerns how you approach your game and how you approach your life. These are two different types of "smarts," and they both affect your athletic performance.

First, "game smarts": the best players have above-average physical skills *and* above-average tactical abilities. That is, they know the game; they know the tactics; they're in tune with what's going on, the flow of the game, and what's needed at any given moment. They know how to position themselves, how to gain an advantage, how to work with teammates; they know what will make it tough for their opponents. And they know what to attempt and what *not* to attempt.

For example, in baseball, a relief pitcher with only an average fastball doesn't try to overpower an opposing slugger who feasts on fastballs; the pitcher nibbles the corners of the plate and tries to entice the hitter to go for off-speed pitches.

If you're a cornerback in football and you're assigned to one of the fastest receivers in the state, you don't play him tight in hopes of intercepting a pass; you respect his speed and play off him a bit.

In soccer, you don't try to score from midfield, no matter how open you are and how strong your leg is; you look to set up a teammate downfield, to gain an advantage closer to the goal.

Coaches love players who know what's called for in each situation. Many times these players are team captains and act as "coaches" on the field or court because of their tactical understanding and game smarts.

Then there are "street smarts": some athletes are controlled and smart in their sport but get themselves into trouble away from sports, because they fall in with the wrong crowd, listen to the wrong influences, or don't have a game plan for how to conduct themselves and what to shoot for away from sports. If you don't have a clue as to where you're going or what you're doing in your life outside of sports, it's not hard to be pulled in the wrong direction. Sadly, many athletes have their sports careers abruptly ended because of mistakes they've made on the streets.

Being smart is what this book is all about: being smart in sports and in life. When you put the two together, you've got the complete package.

"Game smarts" come with experience. Watch collegiate and professional games to pick up on how the best players display their tactical knowledge and court or field awareness. Read books about your sport to learn more about its complex tactics, and ask your coach for other ways that you can improve your understanding of the game.

"Street smarts" come with knowing who you are, what you're about, and having respect for and confidence in yourself. Your game plan for life beyond sports is the topic of the next chapter.

Achieving excellence in sports is an ongoing process. Focus on your gradual and continual improvement; don't expect it to happen overnight. Celebrate your victories and achievements as they come; enjoy the moment. Too often an athlete's moment in the sun is just that: a moment. Work hard, take pleasure in the work and the accomplishments and the team camaraderie, and never stop trying to improve your athletic abilities.

As you work on your athletic abilities, don't neglect the other areas of your life. That's all too easy to do, and such neglect has a price to be paid.

Let's move on, then, to excelling in life.

2

EXCEL IN LIFE

MIA HAMM: CHAMPION ON AND OFF THE FIELD

Mia Hamm's impact on soccer has been described by Nike Chairman Phil Knight as similar to the impact Michael Jordan has had on basketball, and Tiger Woods on golf.

That's not an empty superlative Knight is throwing around. Hamm is widely recognized as the world's best all–around women's soccer player. Her list of accomplishments is long indeed (see the box below).

Mia Hamm Highlights

She is the youngest woman ever to play with the U.S. National Team, debuting with the team at age fifteen.

She was the first-ever three-time U.S. Soccer Athlete of the Year, male or female (1994–96). She was also named U.S. Soccer's Female Athlete of the Year for those three years.

She was a member of the U.S. Women's National Team at the 1996 Olympics, helping to secure the gold medal in front of eighty thousand screaming fans in Athens, Georgia. That's the biggest crowd to ever witness, firsthand, a women's sporting event.

During the 1996 Olympics, she sprained her ankle against Sweden in the first round, but fought through the injury to lead the United States to the gold medal.

She helped the United States take home the 1999 Women's World Cup championship, playing in front of 40 million viewers and playing to sell-out crowds in Giants Stadium and the Rose Bowl.

She played several minutes as goalkeeper in the World Cup against Denmark in Sweden in 1995, replacing the regular goalkeeper, who had been ejected.

Mia Hamm—getting it done on and off the field.

The list of accomplishments could go on and on. That she fought through injury to play a pivotal part in winning an Olympic gold medal, and that she played goalkeeper when her team needed her to, attest to her willingness to put everything on the line for her team, and to put her team first.

But Hamm, who graduated from the University of North Carolina in 1994, doesn't stop there. While she has done more than her part to elevate soccer in the United States with her on-field play, she has accomplished just as much off the field.

She created Hamm's Heroes, a program that recognizes and rewards deserving children with a full day of excitement at one of her Washington Freedom games in the Women's United Soccer Association. She is as tireless in her devotion to charitable and community causes as she is to attacking the opponents' goal on the field.

Perhaps most significant in her off-field activities is her creation of the Mia Hamm Foundation, which is dedicated to raising awareness and funds for bone marrow disease research (her brother, Garrett, died in 1996 from aplastic anemia) and to encouraging young female athletes. Her goal, she says, is to leave a positive and lasting legacy in the research of bone marrow diseases and for every female athlete to have the opportunity to play the sports they love.

It's no wonder that *Esquire* magazine named her, in 1997, one of the "100 Best People in the World."

Hamm's vision for life has always included soccer, and it has always been much larger than soccer. As Phil Knight said, she has made a tremendous impact on the sport, especially for women.

But the impact she is making off the field indicates that she knows how to move quite well without the ball. Her approach to life makes her a winner on and off the field.

LEARN TO MOVE WITHOUT THE BALL

In most sports, as in soccer, there is continual *transition* between offense and defense. The teams that have strong transition games are, by and large, the most successful teams. In basketball, the Duke Blue Devils have long been known as a great transition team, playing ferocious defense and converting turnovers into instant offense and easy baskets before the opponents can transition back to defense.

In one sense, sports is about continually adapting from one situation to the next, always knowing how to act and react to gain and maintain the advantage.

It's no different in life.

In fact, much of this book is focused on helping you develop your transition game, from sports to other areas of your life. Many great athletes succeed in sports but fail in life; they're like shooting stars whose brilliance is noted for a moment and then they're gone. There are also many great athletes who have made it big in sports and who have gone on to achieve great things in their lives beyond sports. They've learned the secrets of *transitioning* their success, of applying what made them successful in sports to do well in other endeavors. These people are not "here today, gone tomorrow"; their stars keep shining brighter and brighter, even when they're removed from the playing fields and courts.

Their transition from sports to business was like a Duke fast break off a turnover: swift, seamless, powerful, effective.

So what do these former athletes know that other, less successful former athletes don't?

For one thing, they understand and apply the same principles that made them successful in sports to their whole lives. I encourage you to reread Chapter 1 and consider how you can apply those principles not only to sports but to life in general.

For another thing, these athletes apply the following five principles to moving without the ball. These principles have much in common with what I presented in Chapter 1—so if it sounds like you've heard these points before, you have. Here, though, you'll consider them from a different angle, one that will help you shape your life beyond sports. Here they are:

1. Know your passions and abilities.
2. Expand your vision beyond sports.
3. Set and move toward goals.
4. Learn from others.
5. Make the daily choice.

Let's take a closer look at each one.

Know Your Passions and Abilities

All the points in this chapter really boil down to one: don't short-change yourself, don't sell yourself short. Don't tell yourself that your passions and abilities begin and end with sports.

Passion and ability are crucial components of success. It's not wrong to be passionate about sports, but you limit yourself if that's all that you're passionate about.

How do you explore your passions beyond sports? Begin by gravitating to what interests you. Maybe it's music, as for Mike Reid, who was an All-Pro defensive tackle for the Cincinnati Bengals in the 1970s—and a great concert pianist. He expanded his career to writing songs for country music stars, including Willie Nelson, Ronnie Milsap, the Judds, Lorrie Morgan, and many others. Reid is as passionate about music as he was about football—and he has played his passion out in a long and successful career in music.

Maybe it's writing, or business, or something in one of the sciences.

Maybe it's genetic engineering. Don't laugh: eighteen-year-old Tevis Howard of Atherton, California, developed a novel treatment for multiple sclerosis. He found a way to mass-produce a human protein needed to fight the disease.

Or maye you're into technology, like Paul Scandariato of Cary, North Carolina. Paul is a teenager who has his own full-time business and who, at age thirteen, founded Intelli Innovations, a software development and consulting company. He has a six-figure income.

The point is these people have explored, and continue to explore, their abilities and interests beyond sports. In the last two examples, they aren't waiting until they're in their twenties or thirties before testing their abilities.

Read about your interests, gain knowledge in them, talk to people in the associated fields. Learn what kinds of opportunities are out there, what kinds of career paths are available. Explore. Test yourself. Find summer internships or jobs that give you a taste for what you're interested in.

Be proud of your abilities and accomplishments in sports, and don't neglect your potential to achieve more as an athlete. At the same time, know that you have more to offer to the world, more to explore. You need to understand yourself, what motivates you, what interests you, what capabilities you possess. From that self-understanding you can begin to form a vision for yourself beyond sports.

> The better you know yourself—the better you know what's most important to you and what you're confident in and capable of—the freer you'll feel to explore your interests beyond sports. Give yourself the leeway to fail, to explore what might turn out to be dead ends. The real mistake is not in failing at something new, but in not attempting it in the first place. Hold on to your passions and let them propel you forward.

Expand Your Vision Beyond Sports

Am I saying it's wrong to focus on a vision in sports, to have lofty goals to shoot for? Not at all. As I said in Chapter 1, I encourage you to form a vision for yourself in sports, to have goals for yourself as an athlete, to constantly work to grow and improve your athletic abilities.

Just don't stop there.

Take that same enthusiasm you have for sports and transform it

PETER UEBERROTH: A Passion for Sports

Peter Ueberroth loved sports, especially football and baseball. He was moderately talented as an athlete, but he used that talent to gain a water–polo scholarship to college—the only way, he said, he'd get to go to college. And he used his education and talents to stay close to sports—not as a player, but as an executive and entrepreneur.

Ueberroth never starred in sports, but he stuck around sports in an impressive fashion: he turned the Olympics into a profitable event; he was Major League Baseball's commissioner in the 1980s; and in 1999, he led a group that purchased golf's prestigious Pebble Beach for $820 million.

Peter Ueberroth—using his talents to stay connected to sports.

into a successful life beyond the playing fields. Every athlete—no matter his or her skill—has to have a vision beyond sports; life goes on beyond your playing days. You need to embrace the reality of life beyond sports and carve out a path for yourself in a business or field that your talents and desires are suited for.

Speaking of reality, I'm going to lay some on you. Are you ready?

Reality Check No. 1: Only 5 percent of high school athletes go on to become college athletes (and only 1 percent play at the Division I level).

Reality Check No. 2: About 1 in 10,000 athletes go on to become professional athletes.

Consider this: There are 435 players in the NBA (29 teams, 15 players per team). You could be in the top 1 percent of all players in the United States—and not have a ghost of a chance of playing in the NBA. Think of how many great college players never make it. You have to be an *exceptional* college player to be noticed. Many more people win a state lottery of $1 million or more than go on to become NBA players.

Some Revealing Statistics

Percent of African–American high school student–athletes who believe they will play in Division I and in a professional league: 70 percent

Chances of a high school senior male basketball player ever being drafted by an NBA team: 3 in 10,000 (0.03 percent)

Chances of a high school senior female basketball player ever being drafted by a WNBA team: 1 in 5,000 (0.02 percent)

Chances of a high school senior football player ever being drafted by an NFL team: 9 in 10,000 (0.09 percent)

Chances of a high school senior baseball player ever being drafted by an MLB team: 1 in 200 (0.5 percent)

Shannon Mihaltan: Fast Track to Success

Shannon Mihaltan set fourteen school records at Hastings College in Nebraska, winning national championships in three events and being named All-American in ten others. Hardly one-dimensional in track—or in life. She graduated magna cum laude with a degree in elementary education in 2002 and is taking graduate level courses. Her transition to the working world promises to be as smooth as the handoffs she has made on relay teams.

Reality Check No. 3: The average career, in number of years, of the relative few who go on to become professional athletes, is about four years.

For the overwhelming majority of you reading this book, your competitive sports careers will expire when you graduate from high school. For the truly elite (who have both the talent and the grades to play), your sports careers will end when you graduate from college. Even if you're one of those one in ten thousand players who do go on to play professional sports, your career might last only three to five years.

You still need to figure out what to do with the rest of your life. You need to expand your vision beyond sports.

A vision gives you a direction to pursue, a goal to focus on. Without one, you can waste a lot of time and your potential can go untapped. Use your vision as a road map to achieving your full potential in whatever field or interest you are drawn to. And remember, your vision can and will change as you grow older: you don't need to nail down what you're going to do for the rest of your life! You need to focus on a direction that plays on your strengths and desires and that gives you a start.

Ulice Payne Jr.: Seeing 20/20 Through Education

Ulice Payne Jr. is Major League Baseball's first African–American to lead a franchise. Named president and CEO of the Milwaukee Brewers at the end of the 2002 season, Payne oversees the day–to–day operations of the club. Payne was a member of the 1977 Marquette University NCAA basketball championship team.

Payne made the most of his time at Marquette, earning both his undergraduate degree and law degree from the university. Prior to taking over the Brewers, Payne had been a managing partner in the largest law firm in Wisconsin.

Ulice Payne Jr.—using his athletic talent as a vehicle to a law degree and a career in sports management.

Set and Move Toward Goals

As an athlete, you're probably used to having goals in sports—you want to drop your 50-meter freestyle swimming time by one second this season; you plan to increase your volleyball kills per game by two next season; you are determined to improve your backhand stroke in tennis.

Goals come from your vision; your vision is based on your strengths and desires; your efforts to achieve your goals are directly affected by your attitude and approach. They are all interrelated, so you can have a vision for what you want to accomplish, but if you don't have goals to help you along the way, chances are you won't achieve that vision.

Why? Because life gets in the way. Hundreds of things cry out for your attention, but you can't possibly tend to them all—at least not very well. Goals help you make good decisions about how to respond to all the options in your day, about what to do with your time. They keep you from drifting aimlessly. They help you assess your progress toward your vision. Vision is the big picture, goals are the small picture, the stepping stones to reaching the vision.

Goals can help you choose between the urgent—those things that cry loudly for your attention—and the important. Oftentimes the urgent things aren't important at all and can hinder your ability to achieve your vision. Sometimes the important things don't call out for your attention at all, but wait silently for you to tend to them.

Here is an example of how the urgent can drown out the important and slow your progress toward your vision.

Jimmy, a junior in high school who wrestles at 135 pounds, is a gifted wrestler. He's never had to work too hard to win matches and minor tournaments and is beginning to attract the attention of some major college wrestling programs.

In the off-season between his junior and senior years, Jimmy's coach gives him a training program to follow. But Jimmy has never been thrilled with hard work, especially in the off-season. The victories have come easily throughout his career; why should that change?

So Jimmy does a little halfhearted training early in the off-season, then drops his training altogether. He'd rather spend his time with his friends; hanging out with them is much more fun than training.

Jimmy reports to the first practice of his senior season at 154 pounds—and the nineteen pounds of added weight are definitely *not* muscle. He is slow and heavy and not fit to wrestle at that weight. He suffers through a mediocre senior season, and the major college wrestling programs turn their attention elsewhere. The *urgent*—hanging out with his friends—drowned out the *important*—preparing for the next season. The consequence is that Jimmy doesn't wrestle in college, though he truly was gifted in the sport and wanted to succeed in it.

There are three lessons to be learned here:

- Don't let the urgent drown out the important. Set goals that help you maintain your focus on the truly important things in your life.
- Set appropriate goals that will help you achieve your vision.
- Make sure your goals are balanced. Don't focus all in one area.

What are appropriate goals? In my book *Teens Can Make It Happen* I list eight guidelines for setting goals. I'll give you an overview of those guidelines here.

1. Set realistic goals.
If your goals are too difficult, if they are unrealistic in their expectations, then it's easy to become discouraged and give up. Make your goals challenging and difficult to achieve—but achievable.

2. Set meaningful goals.
Your goals will be meaningful to you if they're connected to your larger vision for yourself. You can set all kinds of goals, but if they aren't attached to visions that are meaningful to you, what's the point? And that's the question you'll ask yourself as you stop working on a goal that isn't meaningful.

3. Make your goals well defined.

Make your goals specific. This gives you something clear to shoot for and lets you know when you've achieved it. Define a goal in measurable terms. Rather than saying "I want to focus on my schoolwork next semester," say "I want to have a 3.0 grade point average next semester." You'll clearly know whether you achieved the latter goal. The first goal is blurry and subjective and doesn't give you anything to shoot for.

4. Create goals that motivate and excite you.

It's going to be hard to achieve your goal if it's so dreary that you hate to think about it. Remember, your main goals should be tied to your vision—and your vision is based on your passions and strengths. If your goals aren't motivating to you, you'd better reexamine them.

5. Create goals that follow a logical progression.

You'll recall my description of goals as stepping stones to your vision. You should be able to see the steps along the way. For example, if your vision is served by being accepted into a good business school, some of those stepping stones include getting a high grade point average, studying for college entrance exams, doing well on the entrance exams, researching business schools, talking to your parents and your guidance counselor, contacting the admissions offices at the schools you're interested in, and so on.

6. Fine-tune your goals along the way.

As I've mentioned, your vision can and will change as you grow. Sometimes your vision is changed by internal factors—your own maturity, experience, and success can help you reshape your vision. Sometimes you might change your vision because of external factors—things you can't control (injury, poor health, the company you work for is bought out by another company). As your vision shifts and expands, your goals should change accordingly. Goals aren't set in stone. Part of assessing whether they are realistic and meaningful is making sure they are still in tune with your vision.

7. Set goals that get you moving.

One of the main reasons for setting goals is to propel you forward, to motivate you—and require you—to take action to achieve them. Good goals are the link between dream and reality, and they help you to move your reality closer to your dream.

8. Make sure your goals lead to balance in your life.

Make sure your goals are in balance. Don't neglect your studies in pursuing your athletic vision; the cost is too great. Keep your goals in perspective and set goals in *all* important areas of your life.

Share some of your goals with one or two people close to you—a parent or friend, a coach or teacher. They can help in many ways: by giving feedback on whether the goal is appropriate, by helping you fine-tune it as necessary, by offering encouragement and support along the way, by keeping you accountable.

Bo Jackson: Bo Knows Life

In the late 1980s and early 1990s, Bo Jackson did a series of "Bo Knows" Nike commercials. Jackson knew enough back then to play two professional sports: baseball and football. He is the only player ever to be selected to play in both a Major League Baseball All-Star game and an NFL Pro Bowl game. But Jackson, who won the Heisman Trophy at Auburn in 1985 before going on to play baseball for the Chicago White Sox and California Angels and football for the Los Angeles Raiders, had his playing days shortened by a hip injury (he eventually had hip replacement surgery).

Bo was ready for life after sports, though. His move to life after sports was as smooth as his moves on the football field or baseball diamond. He received his degree from Auburn and

runs a Chicago–based company called N'genuity, which spe-
cializes in food processing and distribution. He also has a deal
with Mrs. Smith's to sell his mother's sweet potato and pump-
kin pies. Bo knew sports, and he has always known where he
was going in life, in sports and out of sports.

*Bo Jackson—Heisman Trophy winner, two-sport professional athlete,
and highly successful businessman.*

Learn from Others

One of the first things successful people learn is they can't do it all by
themselves. They don't know it all; they don't have all the resources
and abilities; they don't have all the experience or wisdom.

But they *do* have enough wisdom to know that they can more easily and more effectively reach their potential by relying on, and learning from, others. As you plan your own route to success, you don't have to sweat and struggle to re-create the wheel. Just take the wheel and put a new spin on it—your own spin, based on your own talents and what you have learned along the way.

And much of that learning can come from observing others, from talking with others, from learning about others' success.

So who do you learn from? The obvious ones are parents, teachers, coaches, guidance counselors. Throw grandparents, aunts and uncles, even brothers and sisters into that mix. Add in leaders from your place of worship, and don't forget neighbors and family friends.

There probably aren't too many surprises on that list. You can also learn from peers—your own friends—and from mentors.

When you consider the possibilities, the list of people you can learn from—and who can, either directly or indirectly, help you move toward your goals and vision—is almost endless.

What can you learn, and how can you learn it? The things you can learn are almost as endless as the people you can learn them from, but I'm going to highlight four main areas:

- yourself
- career paths
- accomplishments
- approaches

YOURSELF

You can learn from others about yourself—your strengths and your attributes. Others see you from a perspective that you obviously can't have, and often this leads to others seeing abilities and gifts in you that you don't see yourself. (Others can also see areas of weakness that are holding you back and that you might be blinded to.)

This insight can be invaluable in helping you understand your strengths and abilities, in gaining self-esteem, and ultimately in shaping your vision and goals.

CAREER PATHS

You can learn from others about career paths in the field or fields that you're interested in. Those who can be particularly effective here include your parents, your guidance counselor, your coaches and teachers, and a mentor. You'll do yourself a great service if you can hook up with a mentor to help guide you in building life skills and learning about career interests. Mentors, through their experiences, have a perspective and a wisdom that can aid you greatly as you consider different career paths.

ACCOMPLISHMENTS

You can be inspired by the accomplishments of others, and this inspiration can lead you to attempt things you otherwise might not have attempted, or to even reshape your vision for yourself. As you consider your own abilities and desires in the light of what others with similar interests have accomplished, you can refine your vision and gain new energy for achieving it.

APPROACHES

You can learn from others what has—and hasn't—worked for them in their own pursuits. As I said a few moments ago, rather than re-create the wheel, learn how others with visions and goals similar to yours approached their visions and goals, and what worked for them and what didn't. This can help you refine your own goals and your approach to them.

> Just as in sports, success in life is a team effort. Constantly be learning from others, and look to surround yourself with those who can offer strong support, encouragement, guidance, and wisdom.

Make the Daily Choice

Success is a team effort, but you are responsible for your own success. That is, it's up to you to plan for it and to go after it. No one's going to serve it up to you on a platter.

Ultimately, your success is in your hands. It's your choice.

Do you know how I define success? It's not in terms of money, though money can come from your success. Here's my definition: *Success is about daily choices that bring you more power and freedom to create and act upon present and future opportunities.*

That doesn't mean success is easy. Some of you are in very difficult circumstances right now. All across this nation, teenagers' lives are greatly affected by broken homes, broken dreams, poverty, crime, drug addiction, abuses of various types, abandonment and rejection, loss of loved ones, and a host of other trials and heartaches. Add to that that the teen years are filled with change and that many teens struggle with their emerging identities as they become more and more independent from the adults in their lives, and it's a vast understatement to say that the teen years can be turbulent and challenging. Amid the daily struggles you face, you also have to consider just what we've been talking about in this chapter: your strengths and desires, your plans for your future, your vision and goals.

That's a lot to sort out for a teen in a turbulent world.

Yet, each day, you have choices to make, some big, but most small. The small choices quickly add up to big ones, though. You choose how hard you work in school, how you relate to your coaches and teachers. You choose who you hang out with and what you do when you hang out. You choose what you eat, how much sleep you get, how hard you work in practice. You choose whether to respect yourself and others. You choose whether to get involved in gang or criminal activity, whether to be swayed by others' desires. You choose your own outlook on the world, your own responses, your own approach.

What do you choose? Which way do you want to head?

I'm not saying the choices are necessarily easy. But they are there to make. And you will make better choices if you are confident, if you accept yourself as you are, and if you value yourself and your abilities and gifts. You'll make better choices if you have hopes and dreams, if you have goals that will help you attain those hopes and dreams, and if you have the type of attitude that I talked about earlier.

Choices have consequences. If you cut class, you'll get in trouble. If you don't study, your grades will suffer. If you don't work in your sport, you won't play as well as you could, and your playing time will be cut. If you allow yourself to get pulled in by the wrong crowd, the consequences can get even bigger.

Making good choices doesn't guarantee that everything will work out, but it guarantees that you will have done everything in your power to make it work out. Most often, when you make the right choices, you open up opportunities for yourself. And when those choices are connected to your vision and your goals, you find yourself moving in the right direction. You find yourself fulfilling more and more of your potential, and in the process expanding that potential. When you are in the habit of making the right choices, you find that five, ten years down the road, you have achieved things you never thought possible. And you can continue to build on those achievements as you continue to make those daily choices.

When your self-identity and self-esteem are strong, when you are confident and assured in your abilities and in your essential value as a human being, when you have respect for yourself and for others, the more likely you are to make good daily choices. You aren't in control of everything that happens to you, but you *are* in control of how you respond to life and of the choices you make.

Make the Choice for Education

In Illinois high schools, between 37 percent and almost 50 percent of both girls and boys are failing the state's annual eleventh–grade tests in reading, writing, math, and science. For

African–American students, those statistics are even worse: nearly three out of four boys and two out of three girls fail their eleventh–grade writing tests.

These kids who are failing now are severely limiting their futures. Don't follow suit; make the most of your education. It *does* matter and it *does* pay off.

When you know who you are and what you're about, what your strengths and desires are, where your passions and interests lie, then you can begin to form a vision for yourself. When you have that vision, you can set goals to bring that vision to life. Your attitude and approach to life, and what you can learn from others, steer you toward reaching your goals. Those goals—and eventually your larger vision for your life—are reached through a series of daily choices that you will make throughout your life.

It's all connected; it's all part of the process of choosing to fulfill your potential outside of sports. It's there, waiting for you. But you have to choose to go after it.

And as I mentioned earlier, there will be challenges along the way. We'll examine some of those challenges in the next chapter.

3

KNOW—AND OVERCOME— CHALLENGES

HANK AARON: HAMMERING AWAY AT CHALLENGES

When Mark McGwire and Sammy Sosa chased Roger Maris's single-season home run record in 1998 (McGwire eventually broke the record with 70 home runs), all of baseball thrilled to the two sluggers' accomplishments and gave them wholehearted support around the league. In fact, when McGwire or Sosa drew a walk on the road, fans would boo *their own team's* pitchers.

Contrast that to the situation Hank Aaron faced as he pursued, in the 1970s, Babe Ruth's all-time home run record of 714. Aaron was booed—often by his hometown fans in Atlanta—and as he inched his way ever nearer the record, he received an astonishing amount of hate mail and numerous death threats.

Aaron began his Major League Baseball career only seven years after Jackie Robinson broke the color barrier. That a black man would break the most prestigious record in baseball—and one held by a white man—was intolerable to a large number of people, especially in the racially charged South of the late 1960s and early 1970s. As Aaron approached the record, he had to hire a bodyguard, temporarily change his living quarters, and register under false names in hotels on the road.

But Hammerin' Hank kept hammering away, and he reached the home run record by hitting number 715 on April 8, 1974. When he retired, he was at or near the top in a number of offensive categories (see the box below).

Hank Aaron Highlights

No. 1 all-time in . . .
>Home runs: 755
>Runs batted in: 2,297
>Total bases: 6,856
>Extra base hits: 1,477

No. 2 all-time in . . .
>At-bats: 12,364
>Games played: 3,298

No. 3 all-time in . . .
>Hits: 3,771
>Runs scored: 2,174 (tied with Babe Ruth)

Years played: 23
All-Star games played: 23
Inducted into Hall of Fame in 1982

Aaron overcame numerous challenges in his career to become one of the most successful baseball players ever. So it shouldn't be a surprise that he has been just as successful off the field, where he has played significant roles in a number of business ventures.

His home run total inspired the name for his corporation: 755 Restaurant Corporation. Aaron, through his corporation, owns four Popeyes Chicken & Biscuits franchises, thirteen Church's Chicken franchises, a Krispy Kreme, and an Atlanta–area BMW car dealership.

Hank Aaron—Major League Baseball's all-time home run leader and twenty-three-time All-Star is an All-Star performer off the field as well.

He is also senior vice president of the Atlanta Braves and serves as vice president of business development for CNN's Airport Network. With his wife, Billye, he is the founder of the Hank Aaron Chasing the Dream Foundation. The foundation provides opportunities for children ages nine through twelve to pursue their dreams in areas in which they have shown ability.

Aaron himself is a testament to a man who chased his own dream, realized it despite substantial opposition and challenges, and transferred that dream to life beyond sports.

RISING TO THE CHALLENGE

Michael Jordan is another athlete, like Aaron, who knew how to rise to a challenge.

When Jordan led the Chicago Bulls to six NBA championships in the 1990s, he was the premier player in the league. He was also the league's premier *clutch* player. Game after game in the play–offs, as the contest wound down to the final possession with the outcome still in question, everyone—Jordan's teammates, the opponents, the fans in the stands, the millions of viewers around the world—*knew* Jordan was going to get the ball. He would take the last shot or draw a crowd and dish off to an open teammate.

Much more often than not, Jordan *would* take that final shot. Those were the moments he worked toward, lived for, wanted more than anything. He'd drive, feint, get his defender off balance, elevate, and for a moment it seemed like he hung motionless in the air and the whole world paused . . . and then he'd release; the ball would float toward the basket, and it would nestle softly in the net, bringing the Bulls another victory on another championship run.

One of the common denominators among great athletes is that they aren't afraid of challenges. In fact, they *thrive* on challenges. They want the ball in the final moments of the game. They're confident and sure of themselves; they know what they're going to do. They use challenges to test their abilities and to showcase what they can do.

Athletes who are prepared to meet challenges on the court or field are a step ahead of others in being ready to take on life's challenges. Sports provide the greatest training camp for life, because so much of what you learn in sports you can apply to larger life. Yet, some of the most successful athletes find themselves not able to meet the challenges that life presents them. They haven't learned how to translate what they learned in sports to other careers and pursuits. For various reasons, they've found themselves not up to the challenge.

Pat Conroy: Learning from Losses

Pat Conroy's father was a marine fighter pilot. Nothing Conroy did earned the praise of his father, no matter how good the younger Conroy was. Pat took up sports in part as a way to earn his father's approval, though it never came.

Conroy was a good basketball player, a point guard for the Citadel who got the most out of his average abilities. His inability to earn his father's praise, coupled with suffering through some tough athletic seasons (he recently released a book, *My Losing Season*, based on his 8–17 senior season with the Citadel), led him to his real calling. He is now known as one of America's greatest authors, having penned *The Great Santini*, *The Prince of Tides*, *The Lords of Discipline*, and *Beach Music*, among other books.

Were it not for his stubbornness and determination in approaching—and overcoming—the challenges he has faced in his life, we likely would never have heard of him. But because he turned his losses into lessons learned, he has had a long and successful career as an author.

This chapter is devoted to preparing you to answer the challenges you'll encounter outside of sports. In doing so, I'll lay out some of the challenges you'll face and guide you in how to conquer those challenges.

CHALLENGES TO MOVING WITHOUT THE BALL

The opponents you face in sports are clearly defined: for the most part, your opponents are the players on the opposing teams you face. You have a game plan for defeating them, and usually you know your opponents' strengths and weaknesses.

The opponents you face in life are not so easily defined. They don't all wear the same team colors, they present challenges at different times of your life and in different ways, and quite often you're not even fully aware of them.

I can't list all the challenges you might face in your life, but I will examine six of the larger ones that you might encounter:

- not sure how to move
- fear of failure
- peer pressure
- lack of education
- lack of skills
- lack of connections

Let's take a look at each of these challenges.

Not Sure How to Move

On a rainy Friday night, thirteen-year-old Karla complains to her mother that she's bored. Her mother brings out a five-hundred-piece puzzle of a clown holding three different-colored balloons and dumps it on a card table in front of Karla. "Why don't we put this puzzle together?" her mother says.

"That puzzle looks stupid," Karla says. "I don't want to."

"Don't want to," her mother says, "or can't? There's nothing stupid about the puzzle."

As they continue their discussion, Karla complains that the puzzle looks too hard, that she can't do it, that she wouldn't know where to begin with such a huge puzzle.

"I'll tell you what," her mother says. "If we can get this puzzle together tonight, I'll buy you that new coat you told me you wanted a few weeks ago."

Karla's eyes sparkle; she has wanted that coat ever since she saw it. "But I'm no good at puzzles," she moans. "We'll never get it put together in one night."

"Not with that attitude," her mother agrees.

"All right, all right. So how do we start?" Karla asks.

"One piece at a time," her mother replies. And she instructs Karla to separate out all the border pieces. They get the border put together. Then they begin working on the inside of the puzzle, one section at a time: the clown's face, his big red shoes, the different-colored balloons. Little by little, piece by piece, they get it put together, with Karla doing most of the work.

"I can't believe it!" Karla says as she looks with pride at the finished puzzle. "We did it!"

"*You* did it," her mother says. "I knew you could do it if you put your mind to it."

• • • • • • • • •

Did you notice Karla's early responses to her mother? They echo what many students say about moving without the ball: *It's stupid. I don't want to. It's too hard. I can't do it. I don't know where to begin.*

Then Karla's mother gave her an incentive: a new coat that she wanted. Suddenly Karla had a desire to complete the puzzle; she began to focus her attention on her newfound goal. She moved out of her comfort zone because she valued the reward for doing so.

With some guidance from her mother, she formed a plan for how to move.

Life's challenges in moving without the ball will be greater than putting together a puzzle—but the approach is the same. You move without the ball the same way you move with it: one day at a time, with a plan in mind, a goal to reach, and the desire to reach it. You see the larger picture, and you begin to piece it together bit by bit. You venture out of your comfort zone, you expand your experiences, you allow yourself room to grow. You build on previous success, and you use the same approach that you have used to get the most out of your abilities in sports.

> To succeed in moving without the ball, you need to be willing to take some risks, expand your comfort zone, and throw your effort and energy into the project or task. Remember, the operative word is move! You won't get anyplace without moving.

Fear of Failure

Did you know that Thomas Edison conducted more than twelve hundred *failed* experiments in his attempt to invent the lightbulb before he finally succeeded? He certainly had no fear of failure! Indeed, Edison's eventual success teaches us a great lesson: There's no shame in trying.

Yet fear of failure stops so many of us in our pursuits before we even get a fair start. What's really sad is it often stops us in the things that matter most to us—we "freeze" over them, because we don't want to fail at them.

Take Hallie Ephron, for example. Hallie's parents were screenwriters. Her sister Nora wrote the screenplays for the hit movies *You've Got Mail, Sleepless in Seattle,* and *Heartburn.* She has two other sisters who are prominently published. Hallie spent most of her life defining herself as anything *but* a writer. Finally, with her children in their twenties, she started writing. And she has produced several best-selling novels, with more on the way. In the September 2002 issue of *Writer's Digest*, Hallie says, "What if I failed? Failure in private is one thing—in the public arena, it's quite another. . . . I think I just got old enough and developed enough of a sense of who I am that it finally stopped mattering what other people think. I decided I'd rather have tried and failed than have never found out whether I can do it."

Fear of failure at its base is groundless, because it's really a hypothetical guess: *I don't think I can do this, so I guess I won't try.* That fear alone is enough to stop many people when they encounter unfamiliar areas or challenges. But how do you know you'd fail if you tried? Equally important, as Hallie Ephron came to realize, so *what* if you fail? Do you think the world is so preoccupied with your successes and failures that it's going to stop and criticize you, or critique your attempts?

Hallie Ephron hit on two keys to overcoming fear of failure: you need to know who you are and you need to stop worrying about what other people think. And you need to be resilient, as Edison was, and not let failure beat you.

Failure is a testing ground, a laboratory, if you will, where you experiment and put your own abilities to the test. You figure out what works and what doesn't, and make adjustments as you go along. You learn about yourself. You become more confident, more experienced, more knowledgeable about how to succeed. The real risk in all this is in not taking the risk in the first place.

> If you are dominated by fear of failure, begin by testing yourself in some areas that are of moderate, but not critical, importance to you. Allow yourself the luxury of being less than perfect. Ease up on yourself, learn to laugh at your missteps and blunders, learn from them, and move on.

D. J. Strawberry: Making His Own Footsteps

Many times we want to follow in our father's footsteps. Not so with D. J. Strawberry.

D. J. Strawberry has made a lot of choices in his young life, choices his famous father, Darryl, didn't make. Darryl chose baseball; D.J., with plenty of talent for his father's sport, chose basketball (he signed a letter of intent in the fall of 2002 to play at the University of Maryland). Darryl chose drugs and alcohol; D.J. chose to stay clean. Darryl chose to rely, for the most part, on his excessive talent, having a reputation for not working very hard; D.J. is an overachiever who has put in endless hours to hone his skills.

D.J. even dropped being called by his given name—Darryl Jr.—because the connection with his father, who has been in and out of prison and other troubles, was too painful. Instead, he has chosen to go his own route. And with the choices he has made, he has a bright future to look forward to.

Darryl Strawberry touched all the bases in baseball but has had several missteps in life beyond baseball. His son D.J. has made better decisions in life.

Peer Pressure

"What are you doing hanging out with him? He isn't cool."

"Everybody who's anybody is going to be at that party. Aren't you going?"

"Nice shirt, dude. You pick that out of your old man's closet?"

Peer pressure can affect anyone at any age, but it's most powerful in the teen years. I don't have to tell you that, right? Peer pressure tries to persuade you in every facet of life: the clothes you wear, who you hang out with, where you hang out, what movies you see, what music you listen to, what parties and social events you go to, how seriously you take school, what you eat, how you talk, what activities you take part in, who you date, how you behave, whether you smoke, drink, or do drugs, whether you take part in criminal activities—and, as they say, much, much more.

Now, reading that list, you might say you don't feel peer pressure in several of those areas. But chances are great you feel pressure from your peers in a good number of those areas—and quite often you aren't even consciously aware of how much pressure you feel.

The point is, it's there, and you have to deal with it. Because if you don't, you're letting others run your life for you. We all want to make our own decisions for ourselves, but we often allow our peers to persuade us to do things we really, deep down, don't want to do.

Peer pressure is the challenge that disturbs me the most. I've seen so many people throw their lives away, or make significant mistakes that take years to overcome, because they couldn't stand up to peer pressure.

Don't give people the power over you to make or to influence your decisions. Keep that power for yourself. Decide your own course of action. In deciding, stand up for what you know is best for you.

Three weapons against peer pressure—and you need weapons against it, because it's a battle—are self-awareness, self-acceptance, and self-confidence. There's strength and power in knowing who you are, in accepting yourself as you are, and in being confident in your gifts and abilities. Together these three weapons give you the courage to make your own decisions and to be comfortable with those decisions, even if they're not popular with your peers.

Peer pressure isn't inherently bad—but when it sways you to make poor choices, you're hurting yourself if you don't fight against it. Having a vision for yourself, knowing who you are, and being confident in yourself—and accepting yourself for who you are—are keys to overcoming peer pressure.

Lack of Education

Education is, of course, big business. As it is with all businesses, marketing is a big part of a college's or university's success. When their sports teams excel, a university's name gets out there. Sports teams are great advertising and marketing vehicles for universities.

So the universities recruit the best athletes they can. The student–athletes come in with a mission to win. The more successful they are in their mission, the more successful the university is in its mission.

Great pressure is put on these college athletes to win. Of course, they are given the chance to get a college degree while they're in school, but in many larger universities the focus on sports and the pressure to win is so great that academic pursuits take a backseat to athletic pursuits—and in many cases, the academic pursuits are shoved out the door altogether.

So players come and go through the college system; they're in the spotlight for a short while and then they're out of it—and quite often without a degree to show for it. Their fifteen minutes of fame are gone before they know it, and all of a sudden they're facing a future with not a lot of great options to choose from. The only doors that open up to them are ones with low-paying, unsatisfying jobs.

· · · · · · · · ·

The message is simple: Focus on your education even as you push yourself in sports. The rewards might not be as immediate as they are in sports, but they're longer-lasting and of greater ultimate importance to freeing you up to live the life you want.

Education leads to picking up job skills and opens opportunities for careers that would otherwise remain closed. It's like the training and practicing you do for sports: without that training and practice, you're lost. It's the same in larger life: without the education, you're lost.

If you don't think education makes a difference, check out these average annual income numbers, according to the U.S. Department of Labor and based on a person's highest level of education:

- some high school, no diploma: $21,400
- high school degree: $28,800
- some college, no degree: $32,400
- associate's degree (two–year college): $35,400
- bachelor's degree (four–year college or university): $46,300
- master's degree (postgraduate): $55,300

In addition, the unemployment rate for those without a high school diploma is two to four times greater than it is for those who have at least their high school diploma.

I talked about peer pressure earlier, and peer pressure can factor in here. Sadly, there's some peer pressure that goes against academic performance. If you feel pressure to just slide through school doing the bare minimum, you have to stand up against that pressure. Remember: it's *your* life, no one else's. Don't be persuaded to go down a path that you'll later regret.

> If you have no desire to do well in school, consider the real-life conse-
> quences. If you do want to do better but are having trouble doing so,
> enlist the help of your parents, your teachers, your guidance counselor.
> Get hooked up with a mentor or a tutor. Ask your guidance counselor
> for help in acquiring better study habits. Keep your long-range goals in
> mind, based on your vision for yourself, and find the help you need to
> keep on track academically.

Lack of Skills

You need two types of skills to succeed beyond your playing days: life skills and job skills.

Life skills are the skills that you need no matter what you pursue. They begin with self-understanding and the ability to form your vision based on that understanding. From there they include plan-ning, goal setting, risk taking, and sticking to your mission or task.

These life skills are aided by your desire and commitment, your ability to be a problem solver, and your ability to face adversity.

These life skills are common threads among people who are successful in life no matter where their focus is: in business, entertainment, sports, medicine, health, law, social services, and so on. I'll address seven key life skills in the next chapter.

Job skills are specific to the jobs you take on. Whether you are a carpenter, a welder, a mason, a banker, an accountant, a stockbroker, a journalist, an announcer, or a sports columnist, you need a specific set of skills to help you succeed in your job. You need specialized education and training that goes beyond high school. If you don't get that education and training for whatever field you're interested in, then you don't move on in that field.

Even as you acquire job skills in a field, you'll find that you can acquire more skills as you go, and advance to higher and higher positions. The most successful people continue to learn and to add new skills throughout their lives. And before they know it, they've carved out career paths, and lives, that bring them satisfaction and fulfillment.

Don't worry if you don't know what you want to do for a career. Keep your options open by doing well in school so that you can continue in whatever field you choose, and by developing the life skills that you need no matter what career path you walk down.

Lack of Connections

You've probably heard it said before: It's not what you know, but *who* you know.

There's some truth to that, but it's not the full truth. Yes, there are plenty of examples of people being placed into positions not based on their education, experience, or abilities, but based on who they know. But there are far more examples of people who have "been

Sammy Sosa: Connecting with Regularity Now

As one who grew up in poverty in the Dominican Republic, Sammy Sosa began life with precious few connections. As a young major leaguer for the Chicago White Sox, he struggled to make connections, too—this time with pitches. Sosa struck out a lot and was traded in 1992 to the crosstown Chicago Cubs.

With the Cubs, Sosa connected—again and again. Enough that he now has more than 500 home runs, four times hitting more than 50 in one season. He won the National League Most Valuable Player award in 1998, the year he slugged 66 home runs and led the major leagues in runs batted in with 158.

Sosa hasn't forgotten his native country. When Hurricane George ravaged the island a few years back, leaving more than a hundred thousand people homeless, Sosa had more than thirty thousand pounds of rice, thirty thousand pounds of beans, and numerous barrels of purified water sent to the Dominican Republic, and he aided in the rebuilding of homes. He also established the Sammy Sosa Charitable Foundation to help improve the education and health standards of children in both the United States and the Dominican Republic.

discovered" based on their education, experience, and abilities, despite their lack of knowing someone who could help them be placed in the position.

The reality is it's both what you know and who you know. You *can* find your way, given your talent, experience, and desire, but you can find your way *quicker* if you have connections. By "connections" I mean people who can help you get a foot in the door, enter into the field you're interested in.

Who are those people?

You might be surprised: almost anyone.

Of course, the best connection is with the person who has the direct ability to hire you. But unless you know a lot of company executives or human resources directors, you're not likely to have that connection.

Someone you know might have it, though: a parent, an aunt or uncle, a teacher, a friend, a mentor, or, later on, a co-worker. Or they might know someone who knows someone. Or you might make a connection through a team you played on, an organization or club you belong to, or your church or school. Connections can stretch a long ways, and they don't have to be direct to work.

Relationships, then, are an ideal way to make successful connections, but you can make connections in other ways: through your education, through your life experiences, through your successes, through your ability to showcase your talents, through your own initiative.

To take the initiative and to showcase your own talents—to be, in effect, your own publicist—takes planning and work. Employers won't come knocking on your door offering you great jobs, but they might notice you if you research and plan how to most effectively present your abilities and experience and show those employers what you can do for them.

> Remember, to make a connection, you don't need to know the president or CEO or human resources director of a company. You just need to know someone who knows someone within the company. From there, you need to be prepared to showcase your talents. This doesn't mean exaggerating your abilities or experiences, but giving people a clear idea of what you want to do and what you can do for them.

CONSEQUENCES OF NOT MOVING

Rasheed was a gifted basketball player, a kid with size and grace and ability and heart. He excelled in basketball from early grade school through high school, where he earned All-State honors. From eighth grade on, he was labeled a "can't-miss" prospect who surely had a bright basketball future ahead of him.

He was smart, too—but not smart enough to apply himself in school. He coasted. Life in the classroom and beyond seemed to be in varying tones of gray; only when he stepped onto the court did life bloom in living color.

Rasheed was accepted into a major Division I school, one with a very good basketball program. He showed great promise as a freshman, retaining his "can't-miss" label for his future years in college. He struggled in school but managed to squeak by. School was a stepping-stone to the NBA; he only wanted to remain eligible to play.

In the summer between his freshman and sophomore years in college, Rasheed tore up his knee. He had surgery and rehabbed as a redshirt during his sophomore year. He continued to struggle with his grades, falling far behind in the number of credits he should have earned.

And he lost his quickness and agility; he was not the same player when he returned for his junior year. He languished on the bench. He no longer was a "can't-miss" kid; he was a sad story that quickly became no story at all.

Rasheed dropped out of school at the end of his junior year. He knew he could no longer play ball, and he felt lost as a student. He had no plan to fall back on. He had always thought he would move *with* the ball and therefore didn't pay attention to moving *without* the ball.

• • • • • • • •

How many times have you heard that a high school player has can't-miss potential—but something happens (poor grades, drug problems, problems with the law, personal problems) that causes him to miss? Almost invariably these can't-miss kids who *do* miss not only miss their potential in sports, they miss it in life as well. They drift off into anonymity, their luster faded, their hopes shattered, their one-time potential now mocking them as they struggle through a life of trouble.

Such kids are paying the consequences of not moving without the ball.

They set themselves up for failure and cut themselves off from opportunities to succeed in life. They are heading toward less satisfying jobs and lower income, if not toward jail. Wherever they are headed, they are not going to reach their potential in life.

No one wants those consequences; no one wants to see his or her potential go untapped. But many young adults set themselves up for such lives because they don't know how to move without the ball and have never really given it much thought.

Don't let that happen to you. I want you to tap into your potential in all areas of your life. To do so, you have to learn how to overcome challenges as they arise.

OVERCOMING CHALLENGES

Toby is a junior in high school. His first two years he was a sub on the soccer team, a striker playing behind a very talented kid who has now graduated. It's Toby's time to step up—if he can do it.

There are a lot of keys to Toby's success, but they can be summarized this way: He has to be *motivated* to step up and take over for the departed star, to learn new skills, and to continually improve himself. He must be *open* to exploring and stretching his capabilities, to working hard. He has to be *visual*—he has to *see* himself succeeding before it happens, and he has to see plays happening before they happen. And he has to be *educated*, knowing the game and his position and his skills and his opponents' skills.

Motivated. Open. Visual. Educated. As an acronym, they spell "MOVE."

And that's what you have to do to overcome challenges.

Motivated

Not many things just drop gently into your hands in this life. Usually when people attain something worthwhile, it's because they were highly motivated to attain it, and that motivation drove them until they got it.

As an athlete, you probably know plenty about motivation. You have a drive to succeed, to improve yourself, to win. It's what propels you through grueling workouts and hundreds of sweat-stained shirts in a season.

Take that same drive to succeed and use it now in your school life and later in your work life. Use it in all areas of your life. Be motivated to learn new skills apart from sports, to test and stretch yourself.

The saying "Where there's a will, there's a way" is true. If you want something badly enough, chances are good you will find a way to get it.

Don't let doubt, fear, uncertainty, or peer pressure sap you of your motivation to succeed beyond sports. Focus on your goal, whether it is to raise your grade point average, to receive an academic scholarship, to learn how to play the piano or work wood or develop a software program. When your focus is sharp and singular—when you are wholly committed to what you are doing, no matter what your friends say or what doubts or fears you might have—you're on the right road.

Girls' Sports: Turning Challenges into Opportunities

In 1971, fewer than 195,000 girls played high school varsity sports, and women received only 2 percent of overall college sports budgets. In 2001, 2.8 million girls played high school varsity sports (an increase of nearly 850 percent), and the collegiate athletic budgets for men and women are now much closer to parity. Opportunities have increased greatly for girls and women in sports and in business.

Renee Powell: Breaking Barriers

Renee Powell is the only African-American who is a member of both the Ladies Professional Golf Association and the Professional Golf Association. In 2002, Powell received the Executive Women's Golf Association Leadership Award, presented annually to a person who has made longtime and outstanding contributions to women's golf.

In addition to excelling on the links, Powell has been a golf apparel designer and a teacher and clinician for various golf programs, served on numerous boards and committees, established her own Youth Golf Camp Cadre Program, and has been extensively recognized for her contributions to the game. She was recently named one of the top fifty teachers by *Golf for Women* magazine.

Open

Life is about continual growth. Grandma Moses, one of America's most famous painters, began painting at age sixty-seven and took up the art seriously at age seventy-six. As the singer Bob Dylan once said, "Those not busy being born are busy dying." The status quo doesn't stay the status quo for long; things change, and if you don't change along with them, you're left behind. You have to be continually moving forward, growing, expanding your abilities and experiences, exploring your interests. You have to be open to new challenges, to new opportunities, to taking risks that will bring you closer to your vision for yourself.

Visual

Athletes can improve their performances through mental imagery or visualization. In short, they see themselves performing well in clutch situations; they see themselves using proper form and executing skills and tactics to successful completion. This puts them

Franco Harris: Still Open to Success

Older sports fans will remember Franco Harris for his role in what is known as the "Immaculate Reception"—plucking a football out of the air shortly before it hit the ground, after it had bounced off another player, and rumbling into the end zone to complete a sixty-yard touchdown late in a 1972 NFL play-off game against Oakland. Pittsburgh, the team Harris played for, won that game 13–7. In fact, the Steelers won four Super Bowl titles with Harris running the ball for them; he rushed for more than twelve thousand yards in his thirteen-year career.

Harris not only resurrected the Steelers in that play-off game; he resurrected Parks Sausages, a Baltimore business that was about to shut down in 1996. Today it is alive and well under Harris's guidance. Harris is also founder, owner, and CEO of Super Bakery, Inc., a maker of high-quality pastries distributed nationwide. Super Bakery is not only a financial success; it provides scholarships to minority students majoring in food science.

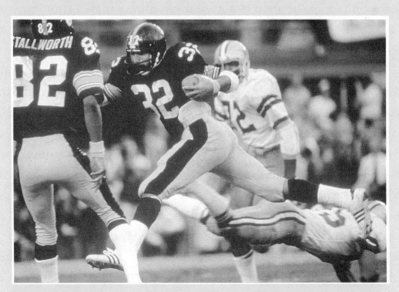

Franco Harris made the most of his opportunities on the field, and has done the same off the field.

in a positive frame of mind, and it also gives them the sense that, when they come upon the situation in the actual game, they've been there, done that. So they have confidence that they can do it again.

People who are successful in life often have the ability to imagine their success before it happens as well. Part of this stems from a solid and positive self-concept; you know who you are and you feel good about yourself. That's half the battle, but only half. The other half concerns your ability to imagine yourself successfully operating in whatever your chosen field is.

Visualization can help you consider the consequences of your decisions. As you play the consequences out in your head, you can form a clearer picture of the likely results of your decision, and you can better see whether that decision is to your benefit.

Visualization can work both short-term and long-term. In the short-term, it can help you achieve better grades this semester. It can help you improve your skills in your sport. It can help you do better in your part-time job or give back to the community by volunteering your time and energy and talent to a cause you believe in. It can also help you in the long run as you visualize yourself running your own business, or being a concert pianist, or becoming a surgeon or a physical therapist or a teacher or a coach.

That might seem like a long way off for you right now, but that's exactly why visualization is important: it helps you keep the big picture in mind and helps you see yourself being successful in that big picture.

Consider Nelson Mandela. A black South African, Mandela was imprisoned for decades because he was seen as a threat to those who upheld apartheid. The word "apartheid" literally means "separateness," and it describes a system built on segregation and racial discrimination. Though Mandela was physically separated from his people for a time, he was never separated from his hope and his vision of a free South Africa. Mandela did not wither in all those long years he spent in prison; his spirit was indomitable as he clung to the vision of freedom for his people, for all those who suffered under apartheid.

And Mandela's will and vision, his strength and spirit, proved stronger than that of those who imprisoned him, and it proved stronger than apartheid itself. He was finally released from prison in 1990, and I had the privilege of visiting with him in South Africa a few days after his release. He was humble, dignified, direct, calm, deeply principled, and unwavering in his pursuit of his vision. In short order, the man who was imprisoned for being a rebel and a threat to his nation was elected president of that nation, and the back of apartheid was broken. In great part it was broken because Mandela formed and retained a strong image of what South Africa should be, and his strength finally won out over an evil system.

Educated

Education is a cornerstone of success. I've said it in other places and in other ways; without education, you can't get far.

If you want to be in business or any professional field, you will be greatly aided by at least a bachelor's degree from a four-year college or university. In many cases, you can't get into a field without a bachelor's degree.

Trade and technical schools might be your route, rather than a four-year university, depending on your desires. Or an associate's degree from a two-year community college can get your foot in the door in a wide variety of fields.

The point is, if you stop your education with your degree from high school, you are limiting your choices.

· · · · · · · ·

Once you learn to move on your own without the ball, you open a host of opportunities that were otherwise closed to you. Then you begin to build skills that will serve you in sports and out.

I call those skills "life skills" because they serve you throughout your life. How to build life skills is the topic for the next chapter.

Julius Erving knows it takes the same thing to succeed in sports and in life: talent, preparation, and execution.

4

BUILD LIFE SKILLS

JULIUS ERVING: THE DOCTOR IS STILL IN

When Julius Erving was in fourth grade, his teacher asked him what he wanted to be when he grew up.

"A doctor," he replied in his typical reserved and modest manner.

Hardly a typical response for a kid who began his life in public housing. Most kids in public housing could be excused if they merely hope to survive into adulthood, much less become a doctor. But Erving was not most kids. He wasn't afraid to dream of greater things. And, guided by his mother, Callie Mae Lindsey, he was able to achieve the seemingly impossible: he kept his feet on solid ground while soaring ever higher on the Campbell Park courts in Hempstead, Long Island, and later on in high school, college, the American Basketball Association (ABA), and finally to the pinnacle: the NBA.

"My mother has been the most stabilizing influence in my life," Erving says. "My dad passed when I was very young [Erving's father was struck and killed by a car when Erving was eleven], and my mother was a central figure to me. She had to raise three children, and she not only put food on the table but instilled values in us that have helped me to this day."

Callie Mae took on the responsibility of raising Julius and his brother and sister by herself. She never missed a beat, never felt sorry for herself, and Julius took his cues from her.

"The character that I possess was instilled by her lessons, her value system, her personal discipline," Erving says. "I learned that to be successful you had to not only try to be a good person, try to do the right thing, try to be success–oriented, but not be ego–driven. I think it's important to try to get on with making your community better, making the world a better place to live, having love in your heart for all people. Don't be so quick to judge people, to think you know all about them. I like to be a guy who sees the glass as half full, not half empty. I like to project positive energy."

Erving starred at the University of Massachusetts, then left school after his junior year to sign with the Virginia Squires of the ABA. Erving later led the New York Nets to two ABA titles. When the ABA merged with the NBA, Erving went to work for the Philadelphia 76ers, playing eleven years for them, averaging twenty–two points per game, winning the league Most Valuable Player award in 1981, and playing a pivotal role in the finals sweep of the reigning champion Los Angeles Lakers in 1983. For a look at some of Erving's career highlights, see the box below.

Julius Erving Highlights

- One of only six players in NCAA history to average more than 20 points and 20 rebounds per game
- ABA MVP (1974, 1976)
- ABA championship with New York Nets (1974, 1976)
- Led the ABA in scoring (1973, 31.9 ppg) and in 1974 (27.4 ppg)
- Five-time ABA All-Star (1972–76)
- Holds career ABA record for highest scoring average (28.7 ppg) in a minimum of 250 games
- NBA MVP (1981)
- Led 76ers to NBA championship (1983)
- All-NBA First Team (1978, 1980–83)
- Appeared in 11 NBA All-Star Games (1977–87)

- Two-time All-Star Game MVP
- One of only four players in pro basketball history to score more than 30,000 career points
- NBA 50th Anniversary All-Time Team (1996)

Fitting of a champion, he also made good on a promise he made to his mother fifteen years earlier, returning to UMass to receive his bachelor's degree in business. His transition from basketball to life beyond was as seamless and graceful as his game. With the same quiet determination, the same level of preparation, the same desire and passion, Erving began crafting his career beyond the courts even as he was still dominating opponents on them. "I've always been a good listener," he says. "I guess I used to be shy when I was growing up, though I wouldn't call myself shy anymore. But I'm still quiet and reserved, more of a listener, and because of that I hear things that continue to benefit me in the long run. The ability to listen, to analyze and assess a situation, are qualities that have been huge in my development beyond the basketball court."

That development includes a stint working with David Stern, the commissioner of the NBA; as an announcer for NBC; as a member of the board of directors of Meridian Bancorp and of the Philadelphia Coca-Cola Bottling Company; and as president of a management and marketing firm. Erving is currently executive vice president of RDV Sports, the parent company of the NBA's Orlando Magic. He has stayed close to home and to the sport that he loves, yet expanded his already prodigious reach.

"Whatever field you choose, your success depends on you acquiring the skills you need," he says. "That includes being open-minded, trainable and teachable, and knowing that the acquisition of the necessary skills is a process.

"Success comes from experience coupled with the proper intellectual energy to learn and absorb and follow the guidelines. You're not trying to reinvent the wheel. People have been there before, been successful. You learn from their success and you emulate it.

"In both sports and business, it's talent, preparation, and execution."

Whether on or off the court, Erving has shown that he has the talent, that he has prepared, and that he has executed. In fact, he has executed with the precision and expertise of a highly skilled surgeon. In the greater sense, he fulfilled his declared intention of becoming a doctor. He operated on the game itself, and he pioneered new techniques of operating. He then took what he learned through basketball to craft a successful life once he retired from the game. As he says, "I felt I could be anything I wanted to be if I put my mind to it and worked hard to achieve it."

GET IN THE GAME

There's no doubt that Julius Erving worked extraordinarily hard to achieve all he did. He also had some skills to work with. He didn't build himself into a legend without having the basic skills to begin with. In sports, you can't get in the game if you don't have the skills.

It's the same in life: you miss out if you don't have the required skills. Here I'll examine seven important life skills that you need to attain. There are other life skills, but if you attain these seven, you'll be building the type of life that is filled with opportunities and achievements, with satisfaction and growth. These are the skills I'll be talking about:

1. Believe in yourself.
2. Challenge yourself.
3. Make learning a lifelong experience.
4. Think outside the box.
5. Be flexible and adaptable.
6. Keep it in perspective.
7. Keep growing.

Let's take a look at each skill.

Believe in Yourself

Albert Einstein and Thomas Edison had dyslexia, a learning disability that makes reading and learning difficult; so does actress and comedienne Whoopi Goldberg. The disorder did not stop Einstein or Edison, and it has not stopped Goldberg from achieving great things in her life.

Jackie Robinson broke Major League Baseball's color barrier in 1947, enduring tremendous criticism, humiliation, prejudice, and discrimination. He went on to become one of baseball's all-time greats and opened the door for other African-Americans to play Major-League Baseball.

Christopher Reeve, a successful actor, broke his neck and became paralyzed in a horse-riding accident in 1995. He has since raised millions of dollars to fund research for the effective treatment and cure for paralysis, and he has made progress with his own condition that doctors bluntly said could never happen.

Pete Gray played a year as an outfielder for the St. Louis Browns in 1945, batting .218. Not too impressive? Consider that Gray had only one arm. His right arm—which he normally threw with—had been amputated, and he taught himself to bat and throw with his left arm.

Harriet Tubman was born to slaves on a plantation in Maryland in 1820. A slave herself, cruelly and harshly treated, she was nicknamed the "Moses of her people" for leading them to freedom on the Underground Railroad. She freed more than three hundred slaves and was awarded a silver medal by Queen Victoria for her bravery.

Different walks of life, different situations, different challenges. But one thing all these people had in common was a belief in themselves and in what they were (or are) doing. Had any of them not believed in themselves, not risen to the challenges they were facing, they would not have accomplished what they did. And in many cases, that would have changed, for the worse, not only their own lives but those of thousands, sometimes millions, of others.

There are countless other stories I could relate of people who achieved things against all odds because they were fueled by their belief in themselves and what they were trying to accomplish. But you get the picture. There's an anonymous poem that goes, in part, this way:

> If you think you are beaten, you are
> If you think you dare not, you don't
> If you'd like to win, but think you can't
> It's almost a cinch, you won't
> Because life's battles don't always go
> To the stronger or faster man
> Sooner or later, the person that wins
> Is the one who says, I CAN!

An interesting side effect to believing in yourself is that others begin to believe in you, too. They see your attitude and self-respect, your confidence and determination, and it rubs off on them. And when that happens, you start to do things that otherwise you wouldn't have dared to even try.

> You can't control the outcome of everything you do, but you can control your effort and your attitude. Check the internal voice in your mind; if it's saying "I can't do this" or "I don't know how to do that" or "This is too hard," turn those thoughts off, because they're steering you in the wrong direction. Tell yourself what you *can* do instead.

Willye White: Believing in Herself—and in Young People

Willye White achieved phenomenal excellence in sports: after all, she is the only American to compete in five—yes, *five*—Olympic Games in track and field, competing in each Olympiad from 1956 to 1972. She is the first American woman to medal in the long jump. She won two silver medals. She is the first American to win the Fair Play Medal (the world's highest sportsmanship award). She is in seven sports' halls of fame. She was a member of five world-record relay teams. She was chosen as one of the 100 Greatest Athletes of the Century by *Sports Illustrated for Women* in 1999.

Always fast during her track and field career, Willye White has never slowed down. She has been a teacher, coach, lecturer, and administrator. She is founder and president of the Willye White Foundation, which is dedicated to developing young people into balanced individuals capable of functioning as productive citizens. Her foundation emphasizes life skills and education. Through her career as an athlete, White developed motivation, determination, tenacity, and a host of other qualities that helped her succeed in track and field and in life.

Challenge Yourself

Lance Armstrong was diagnosed with testicular cancer in 1996. Armstrong not only beat the cancer; he beat the best cyclists in the world for five straight years, beginning in 1999, at the Tour de France bike race. With his victory in 2003, he joined "the club" of only five riders who have won this prestigious event five times. In cycling and in life, Armstrong has faced and overcome great challenges.

All the people in the previous section faced great challenges, too. They were forced to rise to the occasion or to shrink back, their potential unfulfilled. They rose to the occasion.

Hopefully, if and when you're challenged by life's circumstances, you'll find it within yourself to rise as well. But there are times when you can coast along unchallenged by external forces. You're undisturbed, in a routine, no major problems—except for one: you're not challenging yourself. You're not growing, you're not extending yourself. Sometimes you have to raise the bar higher for yourself to achieve more, to learn new things, to open up more opportunities.

You don't have to wait for life to challenge you. Challenge yourself—to learn more, to acquire more skills and experience, to expand your interests, to take on new risks that will help you achieve your vision for yourself. Successful people appreciate what they have, but they aren't willing to rest on their laurels. They continually challenge themselves to achieve more.

> I often hear people say they're bored with their lives, nothing ever happens. The cure for boredom is challenge.

Make Learning a Lifelong Experience

First and foremost, you need your high school education. You'll be doing yourself a great favor by extending that education to attain a two–year associate's degree, a four–year bachelor's degree, or a degree from a technical or trade school. You'll do even better if you earn a master's degree or beyond. The main point is, stick with your education; chart your course and go after it just as you do your sports goals. It pays good dividends in the long run.

But your learning doesn't stop with books or school. Those who achieve the most in life are those who never stop learning. That means you look for ways to improve yourself and your abilities throughout life—through work experiences, through seminars and workshops, through studying and acquiring knowledge on your own.

It's like picking up new skills in your sport to make you more versatile, more valuable. It works the same way with education: the more versatile your education is, the more valuable you'll be seen by potential employers. Then, when you're out of school, continue to learn. Professional players who are successful beyond their playing days do this: they learn broadcasting skills, or how to run a business, or they pick up skills that will serve them in whatever field they decide to go into.

Using Sports as a Vehicle to Education

Sports can provide a great vehicle to receiving a college education. But too often it seems it's the other way around: a college education is seen as a means to play sports and to transition into a professional sports career. Too many athletes burn up their college educations at the expense of gaining a few moments of glory on the college gridiron or hardwood. Unfortunately, it's the athletes themselves who are burned in the end.

Consider this: Forty-eight of the sixty-three universities affiliated with the Bowl Championship Series—in other words, the major football colleges across the country—have a lower rate of graduation for football players than for the general male population of their student bodies. At nearly half of those schools the graduation rate is ten or more points below the school's overall rate. Ninety percent of these schools also had lower graduation rates for basketball players.

A few examples: Over a recent four-year period, Michigan graduated 80 percent of its males, but only 47 percent of its football players. Virginia Tech's numbers were 69 percent and 40 percent, respectively. Oklahoma's were 46 percent and 26 percent.

The point is simple: If you are gifted enough to receive a college athletic scholarship, play hard, give your all to your sport—but not at the expense of your education. Come away with your degree, or you'll come away with nothing but fading, and perhaps bittersweet, memories.

Waiting for experiences to happen to you is like a football team being back on its heels on defense, reacting rather than attacking. Learn to *act* rather than *react*; go after the learning and experiences that will open more doors for you. You can't broaden your horizons from a rocking chair.

Think Outside the Box

"Hey man, what's up?"

"Not much. Same old, same old. How about you?"

"Nothing new."

There's nothing inherently wrong with this conversation—you don't have to have something new in your life every day—but if these two guys sleepwalk like this throughout their lives, then they'll live pretty boring lives, don't you think?

To think outside the box is to stir things up, to imagine the unimaginable—and then figure out how to make it happen. Thinking outside the box calls for creative energy and ideas, demands that you are willing to take some risks, challenges you to try new ways of thinking and behaving. It calls for you to consider old problems in new ways, to figure out alternative solutions to life's challenges. It requires you to *not* follow the crowd, to *not* do the "same old, same old," to *not* do things like you've always done them.

All of our technology—cars, phones, computers, and on and on—have sprung from people who thought outside the box. The technology has evolved over time to the sleek and multifaceted models we have today—aided by not just one or two or a dozen people who thought outside the box, but by hundreds, even thousands. Each person who contributed to the development of automobiles or telephones or computers took the technology and, quite often, its potential uses a step farther.

These people didn't say "same old, same old." They said "What if?" People like this say "This is cool, but what if we could make it even cooler by . . ." and they fill in the blank by thinking outside the box.

Consider a few highlights of the evolution of the car:

1769:   Frenchman Nicolas-Joseph Cugnot builds the first automobile. Cugnot's three-wheeled, steam-powered vehicle has a top speed of about 2 mph and has to stop every twenty minutes to build up a fresh head of steam.

1801:   Successful but very heavy steam automobiles are introduced in England.

1804: American inventor Oliver Evans builds a steam–powered vehicle in Chicago.

Mid-1830s: British inventor Walter Hancock builds a series of steam carriages that are used for the first omnibus service in London.

1860: Combustion engines arrive on the scene. French inventor Jean Joseph Étienne Lenoir patents a one–cylinder engine that uses kerosene for fuel.

1864: Austrian inventor Siegfried Marcus builds and drives a carriage propelled by a two–cylinder gasoline engine.

1876: American George Brayton patents an internal–combustion engine that is displayed at the 1876 Centennial Exhibition in Philadelphia.

1876: German engineer Nikolaus August Otto builds a four–stroke gas engine, the most direct ancestor to today's automobile engines.

1885: Germans Gottlieb Daimler and Wilhelm Maybach mount a gasoline–powered engine onto a bicycle, creating a motorcycle.

1893: American industrialist Henry Ford builds an internal–combustion engine from plans he sees in a magazine. In 1896 he uses an engine to power a vehicle mounted on bicycle wheels and steered by a tiller.

The evolution of improvements goes on and on. Today, computer technology has greatly increased the efficiency and performance capabilities of cars, as engineers continue to think outside the box. In the 1980s the notion that a car would "talk" to its driver was science fiction; by the 1990s it had become reality.

That reality was brought to you by—you guessed it—people who think outside the box.

I had you read a portion of the automobile's evolution for a reason: to consider that in many cases the people who were advancing the technology were doing so by working with *what was already there.* These people generally improved upon the existing technology, rather than created new technology. In most cases, they imagined something *better*, not something *entirely new* (though in many cases the improvements made such a quantum leap that the product could be embraced as "entirely new").

Likewise, I urge you to *build on what you have* and *make it better* by thinking outside your own box. I'm not suggesting that you have to be a creator or inventor to think outside the box, or that you have to venture into something totally foreign to you. If you have little musical talent and no inclination to develop it, certainly it would be "thinking outside your box" to consider a career in music—and it would also be foolish.

Instead, take your own talents and desires and think outside the box to develop and move in ways that will get you where you want to go, that will lead to greater use of your talents and desires, that will take you places that you had not—perhaps until this point—dreamed you could go.

Take a passion of yours, or an ability, and ask yourself "What if?" Force yourself to think outside your normal mode of thinking and consider the what-ifs. You're not bound by your past, your current way of thinking, or others' ways of thinking. You're free to create, to explore, to venture out.

Outside-the-Box Thinking for the NCAA Tournament

What if the NCAA made it mandatory for schools in its basketball tournament to have a 50 percent graduation rate for its athletes to compete in the tournament?

One thing's for sure: the tournament would have a lot of new teams involved. Take 2002, for example: the Final Four teams were Kansas, Indiana, Maryland, and Oklahoma. Of those teams, only Kansas (64 percent) had more than half its players graduate. Indiana (43 percent), Maryland (19 percent), and Oklahoma (0 percent) would not have been eligible for the tournament. (Graduation figures were based on freshmen entering the schools in 1991 through 1994 and graduating within six years of entering.) That's not a misprint for Oklahoma. It's just a sad fact.

Be Flexible and Adaptable

Kris was a good high school volleyball player who worked hard at getting better. After her sophomore year, just as she was learning her team's system and had developed a good relationship with her coach, her father was transferred and she moved to a new school. Undeterred, she went out for the volleyball team there and continued her progress, though she had to learn a slightly different system at her new school.

In college, she decided she wanted to become an athletic trainer and took the coursework to point her in that direction. But the athletic training program was cut at her school, and she transferred into a curriculum designed to prepare her for a master's program in physical therapy.

Her coursework there got her interested in medicine. She finished her premed degree and is now preparing to enter medical school. Things haven't always gone as planned in Kris's life, but she has always adjusted well and come out on top.

•••••••

In baseball, most good hitters even at the minor–league level can hit fastballs. What separates many minor–league hitters from the major leagues is their inability to hit curve balls.

Life might have already thrown you some curve balls—that is, some things you didn't expect or want and that have challenged you. If it hasn't yet, it will. And, just as for the minor–league hitters, if you don't learn how to hit the curve balls, you're not going to get very far.

Said another way, you can plan all you want, but be prepared to be flexible and adaptable, because things quite often don't go according to plan. If you're good at thinking outside the box, then you're less likely to be thrown for a loop when things don't happen as you planned them. Part of being flexible and adaptable is being able to consider alternative routes to the goal, as opposed to giving up because your original plan didn't work.

> The first step toward being flexible and adaptable is realizing you can't control all the circumstances in your life. All you can control is how you respond to those circumstances.

Keep It in Perspective

You're going to win some surprising victories in your life—and you're going to experience some crushing defeats. In some cases you're going to do all you can, and it won't be quite enough. In other cases, success will come so easily to you that you'll wonder why that can't happen all the time. Life has its ups and downs, and you can't get overly excited about the highs or overly depressed by the lows.

Why should you keep it in perspective? Because if you don't, you're not as well prepared for your next battle or contest. You're too busy celebrating your last victory and telling yourself how great you were, or you're too preoccupied with licking your wounds and telling yourself how rough life is. Either way, you aren't helping yourself get ready for whatever's coming next.

The Anaheim Angels kept things in perspective in 2002. They started the season horribly, winning only eight of their first twenty-four games and falling far behind the Oakland Athletics in the American League West. They could have given up then. But they didn't; they turned things around and got things rolling. Then, late in the season, Oakland set an American League record by winning

Cal Ripken: A Long-Lasting Legacy

Speaking of perspective, try this on for size: While Cal Ripken of the Baltimore Orioles was setting his all-time Major League Baseball record for consecutive games played—2,632, starting May 30, 1982, and ending September 20, 1998—other major-league players made more than five thousand trips to the disabled list. Ripken wasn't just durable, he was a great player as well. He is one of only seven players to have at least 3,000 hits and 400 home runs, and he has the major-league record for home runs by a shortstop. The two-time American League Most Valuable Player also holds or shares 11 fielding records, and he started 16 consecutive All-Star games.

Off the field, he started Cal Ripkin Baseball, a Division of Babe Ruth League, Inc., offering instruction to players five through twelve years old.

Baseball great Cal Ripkin helps kids learn the sport in which he excelled.

twenty straight games—surely a crushing blow to Anaheim's hopes, right? Wrong. The Angels focused on their own games and stayed close during that record streak by winning sixteen games during that same span. They were the wild-card team in the play-offs, and though they were the underdog in every postseason series they played, they swept through the American League play-offs and beat the San Francisco Giants in the World Series.

The Angels had plenty of highs during the season, and plenty of lows as well. Yet they maintained an even keel and focused on what was in front of them, on what they could control.

When you keep things in perspective, it helps you to achieve all that you can.

> Focus on what you can control, on the things you can do to succeed. Focus is the name of the game. When you don't keep things in perspective, you lose your focus, and you make things doubly hard on yourself.

Keep Growing

Try to imagine your twenty-fifth high school reunion. You catch up with some old acquaintances and find that they've been doing exciting things in their lives—they've received college degrees, they've traveled, they've lived in different cities and held different positions, perhaps even in different careers. The track of their lives is an upward one; they are continuing to grow, to learn new things, to gain experience, to put themselves in positions to succeed. They have experienced greater and greater success along the way, and those successes motivate them to continue to grow.

Then you meet up with some other acquaintances who still seem stuck back in high school. They think the same way, they haven't gotten out and experienced life, they've been stuck in dead-end jobs ever since they left high school. Whatever plans they might have had for a fulfilling life are long gone. They stopped growing after high school graduation, and life has passed them by.

Kevin Johnson: Man of Faith in Action

Kevin Johnson was always active on the basketball court for the Phoenix Suns. He was a lightning-quick guard who made three NBA All-Star teams, became the Suns' all-time leader in assists and in free throws made and attempted, and scored more than 11,500 points in his career while racking up more than 1,000 steals.

He has been just as active in retirement, building his own business empire (Kevin Johnson Corp., which includes real estate development, sports management, and business acquisitions) and, in the process, helping to rebuild the Sacramento inner-city neighborhood he grew up in. Part of the rehabilitation of his old neighborhood includes a $5 million, twenty-thousand-square-foot building.

Johnson, a Christian, has said he tries to be an example because words without action are just words. He has put his words into action by founding St. Hope Academy, an after-school youth development program designed to give inner-city youths academic tutoring and access to educational opportunities while developing their character and Christian principles.

Former NBA All-Star Kevin Johnson helps underprivileged kids build life skills.

Listen closely: When I talk about success and growth, I'm *not* talking about money. Wealth can be a by-product of growth and success, but I'm not suggesting that money be your primary goal. When you focus on reaching your potential by using your gifts and pursuing your passions, when you live a life that fulfills you and is meaningful to you, then growth becomes a natural process. Don't measure your success by your income. Measure it by how fully you use your abilities and gifts, how closely you pursue your passions, and how, as a result, you continue to grow throughout your life.

> Some people seem stuck in the past. They can't get beyond something that happened, or they fear the future too much to move forward. Learn from the past, build on your experiences, and move on. Live in the present with an eye to the future.

BUILD LIFE SKILLS EVERY DAY

Sports give you the opportunity to build the seven life skills I've mentioned. As an athlete, you have to believe in yourself, at least if you want to achieve your potential. Think about how you perform when you're confident and believe in your abilities, as opposed to when you're unsure of yourself. In which times do you perform better?

Your improvement as an athlete is dictated to a certain degree by how much you challenge yourself. You can go through the motions, but no matter how good you are, that won't take you very far. When you challenge yourself to rise to the next level, then you begin to make progress.

You have to continually learn as an athlete as well. You have to learn about the game, your position, the basic skills, the more advanced skills, the tactics. Athletes are really apprentices on the job, continually learning the skills and techniques that will help them improve.

Donnie Allen Kirskey: Seeing the Big Picture

Donnie Allen Kirskey is a client service representative for SFX, a sports marketing and athlete management company. As such, he works with many top athletes in professional sports. He consults with athletes regarding life skills beyond sports, finances, public image, and related issues that help athletes see the bigger picture.

"These guys don't see the big picture," Kirskey says. "So when the lights go out on the court or in the stadium, they have to go back to their roots, their foundation. They need to have a vision for themselves. I want to see them not only become better athletes, but better people."

Kirskey helps athletes become more versatile in their lives away from sports, more business-minded. "I want them to realize that they have a long life to live and that they haven't even lived yet," he says. "I would like for them to take advantage of the available tools and resources. It's up to the individual to want success on all levels."

Part of that improvement comes from being able to think outside the box and being flexible and adaptable. If your opponent knows your next move before you do, then you had better start thinking outside the box. If you can't adjust to adverse situations, then you better seek help in learning how to be more flexible and adaptable.

Sports also give you the chance to roll with the highs and lows, and to learn how to keep victories—and setbacks—in perspective. You learn to celebrate your wins, but not at the expense of preparing for your next game. You feel down after a loss, but not so down that it impairs your ability to prepare for the next opponent.

Finally, sports give you the opportunity to keep growing. Think about what you've learned about yourself through sports, how you've grown, the trials you've gone through, what you've learned through tough wins and tougher losses. Think about how sports help you plant seeds of hope, dream of victory and achievements, motivate you to work hard and to grow as an athlete.

· · · · · · · ·

So you don't have to wait until you're finished with high school to work on these life skills. Work on them right now, in your own sport, and outside of sports as well. Apply them daily in practice, in games, and in your academic and social life. If you work in a part–time job, these life skills are very applicable to that situation.

In fact, they're applicable to *any* situation you find yourself in. The key is to be aware of the skills that you need to be successful in life, and to continually work at them, just as you do your athletic skills. The race doesn't go to the swift, but to the one who endures and finishes strong.

These life skills will help you do just that. Consider the life skills a set of tools that you can use to build yourself a better life.

Now I'm going to give you another tool that will help you in your endeavors: Success Circles.

USE SUCCESS CIRCLES TO BUILD LIFE SKILLS

Once you learn to move without the ball, you have to keep moving forward. That means looking for ways to improve your educational experiences, your work experiences, your skills, your scope, your connections. It's really pretty simple: if you're not moving forward, you're moving backward. There is no such thing as standing still in this life—if you think you're standing still, chances are good life is passing you by. Don't let that happen!

One way to keep moving forward is through Success Circles. I explain Success Circles, and the whole Success Process, in my book *Teens Can Make It Happen* and I encourage you to consult it for a fuller explanation. But let me briefly explain here what Success Circles are and how you can make them work for you.

A Success Circle involves the things that matter most to you. You could have any number of Success Circles, such as Personal Development, Sports, School, and so on. Three Success Circles that can cover a lot of territory for you are Education/Personal Development, Career, and Relationships/Community.

What do you do with your Success Circles? You list the things within them that you can control, the things you can work on to improve in each area, things you can do to better your life. Let me give you an example. The diagram on the next page illustrates what your Success Circles might look like if you're an athlete who likes math and is considering a career in accounting.

· · · · · · · ·

Why take the time to do this? Because it helps you to focus your thoughts, consider what's really meaningful to you, and take steps toward reaching your vision. It reminds you to expand your horizons, to explore new territory, to take some risks. It also helps you remember that if you want to get from here to there, you have to take some steps in between. Your growth and development don't just happen because you want them to happen.

You are responsible for the direction your life takes. Your Success Circles will not only remind you of that but also help you move in the direction that you want to go.

Plot out your own Success Circles. Don't be too critical of yourself as you go; just brainstorm in the important areas (I do suggest at least starting with the three circles I mentioned: Education/Personal Development, Career, and Relationships/Community). List as many goals and ideas as you can.

Then return to your lists and refine them if necessary. Shape them so that they are focused, sharp, and meaningful to you. Your Circles should both inspire and guide you. Make your lists specific enough that you will know if you've accomplished what you've set out to do. Then set out to do the things that you think will make your life fuller, richer, better.

Return to your Success Circles often. Don't fill them out once and

Education/Personal Development:

- Take a risk—try out for a school or town play.
- Get a 3.0 GPA this semester.
- Stick to off-season training schedule.
- Go on my class trip.
- Keep a journal about my goals and how to make them happen.

Career:

- Meet with my guidance counselor to talk about colleges and career choices.
- Find a mentor who is in the financial field.
- Get a summer internship in a local accounting office.
- Take advanced calculus next semester.
- Explore, through the Internet and other means, the variety of opportunities available in accounting and finance.

Relationships/Community:

- Volunteer through a local organization.
- Be more consistent in my relationships with my friends.
- Volunteer at the local shelter.
- Give my coach my full support and effort.
- Encourage Damon, who's struggling in school.

forget about them. Use them to keep you moving—moving without the ball, toward a bright future.

As you move toward that bright future, don't forget to learn from others who have gone before you. That's what the next chapter is about.

5

ACHIEVE YOUR PERSONAL AND CAREER GOALS

SERENA WILLIAMS: EYES ON MANY PRIZES

It might come as a surprise, but Serena Williams is about more than tennis.

The surprise is understandable, because Serena, along with her sister Venus, took the tennis world by storm in the late 1990s and continues her domination of major events (see box below). In 2002, Serena won three of the four Grand Slam singles events, taking the French Open, Wimbledon, and the U.S. Open. (Serena was forced to withdraw from the fourth event, the Australian Open, after twisting her ankle in the semifinals.)

Serena Williams Highlights

Grand Slam Singles Titles

2003: Australia Open, Wimbledon

2002: French Open, Wimbledon, U.S. Open

1999: U.S. Open

Grand Slam Doubles Titles

2001: Australian Open

2000: Wimbledon

1999: U.S. Open

Serena Williams sets—and achieves—huge goals in tennis and in her life beyond tennis.

In 1997 Serena lowered her ranking from No. 453 in the world to 304. She jumped to No. 100 after beating Mary Pierce and Monica Seles at the Ameritech Cup in Chicago, and in 1999, at the age of seventeen, she defeated Martina Hingis in the finals of the U.S. Open, becoming the first African–American woman since Althea Gibson in 1958 to win a Grand Slam singles title. That was also the year that she first beat older sister Venus, in the finals of the Grand Slam Cup in Munich. At the end of that year, Venus was ranked third in the world, Serena fifth.

The following year, Serena and Venus teamed up to win the Wimbledon doubles title and the U.S. Open doubles championship. They also won the Olympic doubles title in the 2000 Games in Sydney.

In the 2001 U.S. Open, Serena met Venus in the finals—the first time sisters had met in a Grand Slam final since 1884. Venus won that title, but in 2002 her younger sister defeated her in the finals of the French Open, Wimbledon, and the U.S. Open. In 2003, Serena defeated Venus in the finals to win the Australian Open title and her second Wimbledon crown, and together they took the Australian Open doubles crown.

With so much achieved on the court, you'd assume Serena has no time for other interests. This is hardly the case.

Serena has been a model, she has a major endorsement with Puma, she attended the Art Institute of Florida along with Venus, where they studied fashion design (Serena has her own line of clothing), and she has found time to pursue her interests in acting (she's done commercials and has made a few cameo appearances in TV shows and movies). She told the *East Valley Tribune* in Mesa, Arizona, "I know I can work harder, I know I can play tennis and act and model and do all these photo shoots."

Serena creates huge goals—such as going undefeated for the whole year—and then sets out after them, knowing full well that they are difficult to achieve and she might fall short. Her reasoning is that the higher the goals she sets, the more she will achieve. She thinks the same way on the court and off the court.

"I've never considered tennis as my only outlet," she told the *Los Angeles Times*. "I've always liked doing different things when I was younger. I just never really liked focusing on tennis. I do see myself as a crossover."

With Serena's determination, confidence, charisma, and abilities, it's hard to imagine her not achieving her goals, whether in or out of tennis.

WHICH WAY ARE YOU MOVING?

Brandon was a young man with a dream: he was going to win an Olympic gold medal in wrestling. He had been wrestling since he was nine years old and had always excelled, and he worked hard to stay on top.

He won a state championship as a senior in high school and

went on to one of the top wrestling programs in the nation. In college he would get up at 5:00 A.M. to work out on his own before attending the grueling afternoon sessions with the squad.

Brandon wrestled well in college, though not quite as well as he had planned. The competition was stiff and he was wrestling against the nation's best in his weight class. Sometimes he won, sometimes he lost.

After his senior year, he also wrestled well at the Olympic trials, but not quite well enough to make the Olympic team. He returned home, his dream at least momentarily shattered. He was twenty credits shy of graduating, but losing at the trials sapped all his motivation. He didn't return to school to finish his degree and ended up shifting from low-paying job to low-paying job, never feeling satisfied. Though he had achieved significant success as a wrestler, he had an athletic hunger that hadn't been filled, and he didn't know how to transfer that hunger elsewhere.

. . . .

Like Brandon, all successful athletes are hungry. Certainly, skills and the other attributes I've talked about are of vital importance to their success, but what can separate athletes who are successful for a career from ones who are successful for a season or for a few games is hunger. The truly successful athletes are never satiated, never filled. They know they can *always* improve, *always* achieve more. They also know that hunger can be used in more than just sports.

If hunger is their driving force, personal and career goals act as their compass. They set goals that move them in the right direction. They use those goals to get from point A to point B—and then to navigate to point C, point D, and points beyond.

And as they reach each individual goal, it moves them one step closer to their larger goals, toward a life of greater fulfillment and deeper meaning. These goals help them move in a definite, logical, planned direction. (Understand that their direction can change along the way as more possibilities open for them—the main point here is that they *move* toward good possibilities in their lives and then choose *better* possibilities as they arise. As they move, they expand their possibilities.)

They don't wait for life to haphazardly come to them—they go after life.

Does that mean they achieve all their goals? No. Does that mean they never experience bumps along the way, failures, or run into some dead ends? No. Does that mean they are untouched by tragedy, by trouble, by trials that test them? No.

It means that they have a plan, and that plan is moving them in the right direction, and because they have an end result, an end goal in mind, they are able to adjust when they need to, to put it in reverse when they find themselves on a dead-end road, to find the right road again that will keep them moving toward their destination.

And so it should be with you. You need to have personal and career development goals in place to get you moving in the right direction, to keep you moving, and to let you know how you're progressing. The alternative is to drift along, to go wherever life takes you.

Unfortunately, life can take you down some pretty mean streets and dead-end roads if you don't steer it otherwise.

We're all moving one way or another—life doesn't stand still, and neither do we, even if we try. Are you moving forward or backward?

NINE STEPS TO MOVING FORWARD

The first thing to know is that you're not insulated in school—that is, what I'm talking about doesn't start once you get out of school. You're in the midst of it; you're moving forward or backward right now.

The second thing to know is that there is a connectedness to these goals and to how you live your life. What you do today counts for tomorrow; what you sow now you will reap later. What you do today, tomorrow, next week, next month *matters*.

And that's tremendous to know, because it gives you some control over your life, some say over your direction, some motivation to really know your abilities and what you want out of life and to plan how to get the most out of yourself and out of your life.

But it's up to you: you set the pattern. You develop the habits, the work ethic. You set your tone, your attitude, your approach. You decide how hard you want to work, what risks you want to take, what you want to achieve, how you plan to achieve it.

You are doing all this now, in school, and it will carry over after school days into your professional and personal life as an adult.

So how do you move forward? In *Teens Can Make It Happen* I defined nine steps to success. While I won't go into the full detail that I did in that book, I'll give you a clear overview of those nine steps and tell you how you can apply them to help you keep moving forward in your own personal and career development.

Step 1: Check Your ID

This step is foundational. As I said in Chapters 1 and 2, you need to know your passions and abilities, what makes you tick, what the influences are in your life, why you act and think the way you do. In short, you need to know *who* you are before you can begin to plan *what* you want to accomplish.

In your sport, you know your position, your role on the team, your strengths and weaknesses, and what you want to achieve. You need to know the same foundational issues that pertain to your personal and career development apart from sports as well. Based on your strengths and your desires, you can form personal and career development goals that will help you live a fulfilling life. But you need to know your strengths and desires before you can form your goals.

This ties in with what I've said earlier: Those who succeed are the ones who dare to dream, who put in the work, and who build on their abilities so that they can apply them in a variety of ways. They know how to tap into their potential because they know who they are and what they want. And this helps them with the next step, which is just as critical as this step.

Never downplay your potential or your abilities. Most people are capable of much more than what they initially think. Your goal here should be to explore all your strengths and to uncover hidden abilities.

Step 2: Create a Vision

I've talked about vision as well. As an athlete, you have dreams and aspirations; you have an ideal in mind for what you'd like to achieve, and based on that ideal, you have at least some sense of how you need to move forward to achieve that ideal.

It works the same way with your personal and career development. As you expand your vision beyond sports, and consider how to apply your skills and desires in other ways, you begin to see opportunities that were there all along but that you hadn't noticed because you were perhaps solely focused on sports.

Kurt Warner: Having a Firm Foundation

Back when no one but family and friends knew who Kurt Warner was, Warner had no doubts about his own identity. Bolstered by his firm faith and a belief in his abilities as a quarterback, Warner arrived late on the NFL scene. He didn't start for the St. Louis Rams until he was twenty-eight years old, but as a rookie in 1999 he threw 41 touchdown passes, accumulated 4,353 passing yards, and earned a quarterback rating of 109.3. Warner and the Rams won the Super Bowl in 2000, completing their storybook season, and Warner has continued his excellence as quarterback for the Rams.

Off the field, Warner founded with his wife, Brenda, the First Things First Foundation, a community outreach program designed to impact lives by promoting Christian values and providing opportunities and encouragement for growth.

You are a multifaceted person with talents that can be applied in a variety of ways. Here's where thinking outside the box—which I talked about in Chapter 4—comes into play. Certainly, if you don't work at it a little, consider various ideas, and explore your own strengths and desires and how you might apply them, then your vision will be limited—or maybe nonexistent. Maybe you can't see yourself doing *anything* other than sports, because that's all you want to do.

If that's the case, you are *vision-impaired* and need to change your way of thinking, because as I've said earlier, even star athletes need a vision for what they're going to do beyond their sports careers. You're going to have most of your life left *after* you've completed your sports career, and if you don't have a vision for what you can and want to do, chances are good that you won't be very happy or fulfilled in whatever it is you fall into.

So, explore. Be creative. Think outside the box. Be confident in your abilities, embrace your dreams, and shape a vision for yourself. That vision will help you achieve your personal and career goals, especially as you apply the next step.

> You probably know the importance of visualization in sports. For instance, good free-throw shooters visualize their proper technique and the ball going in before they shoot; this helps them succeed. The same principle applies to other areas of your life as well. You can help yourself greatly by seeing yourself being successful in whatever your venture is.

Step 3: Develop Your Travel Plan

From your self-understanding and your vision, you can form what I call your "travel plan"—the best route to take to get from here to there. These are the specific steps you need to take to realize your vision, the goals you need to achieve along the way.

In sports, a travel plan might look like Jeff's. Jeff is a freshman miler on the track team in high school. He wants to earn All-State recognition by the time he's a senior and receive an athletic scholarship to college. He has run a 4:43 mile as a freshman. His goals for the next three years are 4:30, 4:20, and 4:10. To get there, he plans not only to run with the track team in the afternoons but to get in extra mileage on his own in the mornings, and to work just as hard in the off-season as he does in season. In fact, he has specific mileage goals and time goals for his personal runs and his off-season training. He also plans to lift weights to gain strength, and to eat the right foods to fuel his body. And he is continually reading up on the latest training methods and routines, adapting them to his personal training. He also has goals of being conference mile champ three years in a row, beginning with his sophomore year, and of placing high in the state meet beginning with his junior year.

Jeff has a very definite plan in place, with markers along the way to help him know how he's progressing. He's not leaving anything up to chance. He's learning about training methods as he goes, he's applying what he's learning, and he's set some lofty but reachable goals that keep him focused.

All of that is excellent. Now Jeff needs to develop the same type of plan for his personal and career development. Beyond track, what does Jeff want to do? What goals will help him move toward the vision that he creates for himself? What steps will he have to take to move toward *those* goals?

Athletes like Jeff don't need to give up their vision for athletic success; they need to continue to focus on that vision and work hard toward achieving it—and pull back a bit, so they can gain the larger view and realize that there are challenges beyond sports that are just as great, or greater, awaiting them. They need to develop the plan to overcome their challenges not just in sports but in all of life.

Those challenges, of course, aren't easy. But if you are a prepared driver, you have some tools to help you either prevent or fix breakdowns as you travel on the road toward your vision. And you have some rules of the road that will help you steer clear of trouble.

Quite often, what stops us from attempting to achieve a difficult goal is that we haven't thought through the process of how we can attain that goal. The goal is formidable and the steps to take are vague. When you break a goal down and figure out step by step what you have to do, it doesn't seem so formidable anymore, and you can just focus on the smaller steps you need to take.

Robin Roberts: Setting Ever-Higher Goals

Robin Roberts, ESPN commentator on *SportsCenter* and news anchor for ABC News's *Good Morning America*, was quoted in the spring 2002 issue of *The Women's Sports Experience* as saying her greatest accomplishment was that she set a goal for herself and accomplished it.

Roberts was a standout basketball player for Southeastern Louisiana University, where she graduated magna cum laude in 1983 with a degree in communications. She worked at TV stations in Biloxi, Nashville, and Atlanta before landing with ESPN in 1990. She has received numerous journalism awards and has covered some of the biggest events and interviewed the biggest personalities both in and out of sports as she has taken on increasingly greater responsibilities. There is no doubt that the type of goal setting she learned from her days as a player continues to serve her well in her career today.

Step 4: Master the Rules of the Road

We've already talked about some of the tools you can use to help you achieve both in sports and out of sports: determination, willpower, imagination, balance in life between sports and other facets. You've used these tools all along in your athletic endeavors;

now you need to expand that usage to help you form personal and career development goals.

As you do, you also will benefit by developing some rules of the road; these will guide you along the way. Your rules have to come from yourself, because you know what will benefit and motivate you the most, but an example of a set of rules is this:

1. *Be honest.* Build trust in your relationships; be a person that others can count on to come through as promised—and one who can admit failure when it happens.

2. *Do the work that is required.* What you put into any project or goal or plan directly affects what you get out of it. Sustained success, whether in sports or in any other area, isn't easy. But it's possible, if you are willing to do the work.

3. *Maintain a positive attitude.* When you focus on negative thoughts, negative relationships, and negative talk, you put yourself in a prison of your own choosing. Focus on what you can do and don't alter your attitude based on your circumstances. It's easy to be positive when things are going right; those who achieve great things do so in part because they maintain a positive attitude and outlook when things are going wrong.

4. *Take the time to think things through.* This aids you in thinking outside the box, in creating your vision, in developing your travel plan, and in every aspect as you make decisions from day to day. Think about the consequences of your words, your attitude, your behavior. Are they moving you closer to your goals or farther away from them? Many student-athletes focus on sports and go on cruise control in other areas of their lives. Think about what you're doing, because as I said earlier in this chapter, you're either moving forward, toward your goals, or you're veering away from them, moving, in effect, backward.

5. *Look at the big picture.* I mentioned this a moment ago: you need to step back from your athletic goals—not losing sight of them, but stepping back so you can see the bigger picture. There's a larger

life waiting for you out there, but if you don't bring it into focus, you'll leave your potential untapped. In sports terminology, if you don't look at the big picture, you'll find yourself sitting on the sidelines. Don't let that happen! Get into the game.

These rules of the road will come in handy as you begin to consider what risks you want to take in life. When you take risks, you step into your own outer limits.

> We all lose our way once in a while. Having some rules of the road for yourself will help you get back on track without too much lost time or wasted energy.

Step 5: Step into the Outer Limits

Marni was a good tennis player and a good student. She had always received decent grades without trying too hard. In high school, though, she had become close friends with two girls, neither of whom was in sports and neither of whom was going anywhere after they graduated—*if* they graduated.

Marni could have easily gone to one of the state universities. She could have gone to a smaller school on a scholarship and played tennis. She could have gone to the local community college to begin her college education. But she didn't go anywhere. Why? Because she had aligned herself so tightly with her two friends that the thought of growth, of expanding her horizons, of leaving her comfort zone and stepping into her own outer limits, frightened her. She opted for the known, even though the known was a dead-end path. At the age of eighteen, she began coasting.

* * * * * * * *

Sure, you can coast. You can "get by." You can even fool others—but you can't fool yourself. You won't be happy until you know you've pushed yourself to your limits, stretched your capabilities, taken the calculated risks that will get you to the next level in whatever you're pursuing.

Notice that I said *calculated* risks. Not all risks are good to take; I'm not suggesting that you leap before you look closely at what you're leaping into. But there are times when you simply cannot get to there from here without taking that leap. You figure out what the risk will cost you to take (and what it costs you if you *don't* take it), and then you figure out the best way to take the risk.

By doing so you can begin to expand your outer limits.

Part of this expansion is determined by how well you learn from failure and criticism. Do you turn a deaf ear to constructive criticism? Do you repeat your failures or simply give up if you fail early on? If you answered yes to either question, you are severely hampering your own ability to step into your outer limits, to learn from life and others, and to expand your abilities and life experiences.

One set of skills that will help you become more adept at stepping into your own outer limits is understanding the seasons of change, and knowing when to seek change, rather than just letting it happen.

> Life is *not* risk-free. So you better learn how to take calculated risks, and to figure out what risks are worth taking.

Step 6: Pilot the Seasons of Change

Tisa and Devon were sister and brother, but you wouldn't know it from how they responded to change. Tisa always seemed to be able to roll with the punches, while Devon worried about every new thing in his life, sometimes to the point where he'd freeze up or withdraw.

When their father took a job in Columbus, Ohio, and the family moved to their new city from Indianapolis, Tisa made an almost seamless transition. Friendly and outgoing, she made new friends easily and resumed her athletic pursuits in basketball and softball. Devon, on the other hand, was miserable. More quiet and shy than his older sister, he didn't make new connections as easily and decided not to go out for football, though he loved the sport, because he was intimidated by being in a larger school. He wished every day that his family could return to Indianapolis and his more familiar surroundings.

· · · · · · · ·

Change is a part of life. Everything around us changes, including people, as they grow and take on new experiences and responsibilities. In sports, coaches and players come and go; dynasties crumble; new champions arise. Athletes take on new roles as they gain skills and experience.

Think of how you've grown and matured in the last year or two. People who are successful don't stop that growth once they reach adulthood; they keep on growing, refining their skills, honing their vision. They change in good ways, which is another way of saying they keep moving forward. They don't stand still, because life doesn't stand still. They keep pace.

You'll keep pace as well if you are able to master the four stages of change:

1. Let go of old things to welcome in new things.
2. Stick to plans to change even when you feel anxious.
3. Hold tight during the ups and downs of change.
4. Blossom and grow through change.

Part of piloting the seasons of change has to do with *seeking* change. To do this, you have to view change as desirable, as a good thing. When you seek change, you take more responsibility and control of your life, you move toward something rather than letting things come toward you. And when you have a vision for what you want to do and a plan for how to get there, it's much more likely that you'll willingly seek change, rather than try to maintain the status quo.

Pam Shriver: Hitting Aces in Tennis and in Life

Pam Shriver's credentials in tennis are world–class: 21 singles titles, 112 doubles titles, 22 Grand Slam titles, and the doubles gold medal in the 1988 Olympics with Zina Garrison. When her twenty–year playing career ended in 1997, Shriver didn't miss a beat, transitioning smoothly to the broadcast booth (she is a tennis commentator for ESPN, CBS, and the BBC). The former player, who was recently inducted into the International Tennis Hall of Fame, has her own company, PHS Ltd., which is involved in charity events and is a minority partner in the Baltimore Orioles baseball team. She also serves on the board of directors of the United States Tennis Association.

Pam Shriver has used her experience and success as an athlete to achieve goals in business.

Either way, change is coming. Are you ready to master its stages and turn it into an ally, or do you view it as an enemy?

While it's true that change happens in our lives all the time, I never said you had to go it alone. In fact, to do so is foolish. Choose the right people to help you master the changes as you work toward reaching your goals.

> Status quo is the enemy of growth and achievement. If you stay where you are, you will never achieve anything beyond what you've already achieved.

Step 7: Build Your Dream Team

The original "Dream Team" was the USA Olympic basketball team of 1992, consisting of starters Michael Jordan, Magic Johnson, Larry Bird, Charles Barkley, and Karl Malone. On the bench were NBA greats John Stockton, Clyde Drexler, Scottie Pippen, and David Robinson.

This Dream Team won all their games by an average of forty-four points a game. The closest game they had was for the gold medal, in which they beat Croatia by "only" thirty-two points. America had a dream of a gold medal in basketball, and they assembled the crew to make sure that would happen.

You can do the same—that is, you can build your own Dream Team to help you reach your goals. As an athlete, you well understand the need for teamwork to reach mutual goals and for building trust among those you work with. The same holds true for your individual goals. Yes, you can "go it alone," but I don't recommend it because it's far less effective than defining who can help you reach your goals and then partnering with those people, either informally or formally, to improve your chances of achieving what you hope to achieve.

Who do you partner with? Some members of your Dream Team can be peers; others will be adults (parents, relatives, teachers, coaches, guidance counselors). Your Dream Team should be committed to a common goal, share common values and expectations, and be willing to help each other out. Together, you and your Dream Team need to have a plan to confront and solve the problems that will inevitably come up as you pursue your goals. You also need a plan to help you evaluate your progress.

There's no need to go it alone. When you figure out what you want, then you can consider who can best help you attain it. You don't need tons of players on your Dream Team—you just need the *right* players, the ones who care about you and share your ideals and can offer you guidance and support along the way.

Of course, you'll face plenty of tough decisions as you pursue your goals. Making wise decisions is one of your greatest assets—and challenges.

> Don't be too proud to seek help and guidance. That guidance and help can sometimes open doors that you could never open by yourself.

Step 8: Win By a Decision

Mark was a sprinter on the track team. He was always smiling, always happy—he was everybody's friend. He was friends with kids on the track team, with students who weren't athletes, with students on the honor roll, with students who were struggling in school. He joked around with his teachers and brought a smile to everyone's face. People just liked being around Mark.

One afternoon David and Emilio invited him to a party that was to be held that night. Several other guys on the track team were going to be there, they said (they weren't on the team themselves and were barely still in school). Lots of good–looking girls, plenty of alcohol, good tunes . . . Mark would be the life of the party.

Mark smiled and hesitated. He knew his parents would not allow him to go if they knew alcohol would be present, and he also knew that he would be suspended from the track team if he were caught. But he loved a party and thought maybe he could go and just not drink.

As he was about to say that he would go, though, he changed his mind. "Sorry, guys," he said. "I really can't."

Despite their protestations, Mark held firm. And as it happened, the police raided the party and three members of the track team were suspended. One other student overdosed on cocaine and was rushed to the emergency room.

· · · · · · · ·

You literally shape your life through the daily decisions you make. Yes, the self-understanding, the vision, the plans, the goals are all important, but really what they all lead to is your ability to make the small, daily decisions that will steer you closer to the big picture you have envisioned.

Of course, the vision and plans and goals inform your decisions—that is, they help you make the decisions that will keep you moving forward. The decision-making process is guided by your vision and goals; they work hand in hand.

In other words, you can dream about athletic success all you want and shape a vision around it. But until you decide to work hard in practice, to keep working in the off-season, to hit the weights, and to eat a balanced diet, you won't realize that vision.

In terms of personal and career development goals, you have decisions to make about how hard you study, how much you care about your grades and about going on to college, how you take care of your body, how you investigate potential career paths. Your Dream Team can certainly offer much help and support in these areas, but you have to decide for yourself what you want and what you're willing to do to get it.

Making decisions along the way is one way that you stay committed to the bigger picture, your overall vision.

If you can't decide what you want out of life, and what you have to do to get it, life will decide for you. Wouldn't you rather decide for yourself?

Bryon Russell: Making the Grade in Life

Bryon Russell has been a star for basketball's Utah Jazz for the past ten years now. But he knows there's life beyond basketball, as evidenced by his decision to finish his bachelor's degree (he was three courses short when he left California State University Long Beach to play for the Jazz in 1993). Russell served an internship with the South Salt Lake City Police Department and was awarded his degree in criminal justice. Russell said he was a student before he was a professional player, and that his degree was always important to him.

Bryon Russell—keeping commitments beyond the basketball court.

Step 9: Commit to Your Vision

I said it earlier in this chapter: Sustained success doesn't come easily. In sports, you might get the breaks against a superior team and pull off an upset. In addition, some victories against weaker opponents and some personal achievements may seem to come with little effort.

The occasional upsets and the effortless achievements aren't tests of your staying power or of your ability to commit to your vision. The tests come when failures crop up, when disappointments set in, when challenges arise.

If you want to reach your full potential in life, you have to be committed to your vision for the long haul. You have to commit to bettering your life and not shrink back when you encounter challenges.

You have to keep your commitments to yourself and to others. Celebrate your successes, learn from your losses, and move forward. That's what it's about in sports and that's what it's about in life.

> Those who stay committed are those who achieve the great, and sometimes seemingly impossible, things in life.

Those are the nine steps to success. They're not a mystery, and they're not a miracle cure. They're tools for you to use to better your life, to keep on moving forward toward achieving your personal and career goals.

Some of those goals should be focused on your health and fitness, so let's take a look at those topics next.

6

ENHANCE YOUR HEALTH AND FITNESS

JERRY RICE: GOING THE EXTRA MILE

Jerry Rice is like the Energizer Bunny: he just keeps going and going and going. In a sport where the average career spans about three years, Rice has played nineteen.

To say he's just "played" nineteen seasons is a huge understatement. Who's the NFL's all-time leading receiver in terms of passes caught, receiving yards, and touchdowns in the regular season? Jerry Rice. How about the all-time leader in those categories in the play-offs? Jerry Rice. How about the Super Bowl leader in those categories? You got it: Jerry Rice.

After sixteen seasons with the San Francisco 49ers and three in Oakland Raiders' uniform, Jerry Rice has three Super Bowl rings, one Super Bowl MVP award, eleven straight Pro Bowl appearances, and he was named to the NFL's 75th Anniversary All-Time Team while still active. See the box below for some of Rice's career highlights.

Jerry Rice Highlights

NFL Records

Most career receptions (1,456)

Most total touchdowns (205)

Most receiving touchdowns (194)

Most games with 100-yards receiving (73)

Most receiving yards in a season (1,848)

Most receiving touchdowns in a season (22)

Most consecutive games with a receiving touchdown (13)

Most consecutive 100-catch seasons (3)

Most seasons with 50 or more receptions (13)

First player in league history to reach 20,000-yard mark rushing or receiving

Super Bowl Records

Most career receptions (28)

Most receptions in a game (11)

Most career receiving yards (512)

Most receiving yards in a game (215)

Most career points (42)

Most points in a game (18)

Most career touchdowns (7)

Most touchdowns in a game (3)

Awards

NFL Rookie of the Year Award (1985)

Super Bowl MVP (1988)

NFL Player of the Year (1990, 1997)

NFL Offensive Player of the Year (1993)

Pro Bowl MVP (1995)

The truth is, Rice is rarely *inactive*. He was felled by a knee injury in 1997; he ripped off his splint after having reconstructive surgery two weeks before and trudged off to the weight room. He had a second knee surgery later that year, yet came back the following year with eighty–two receptions and 1,157 yards after being written off as too old, too beat up. Barry Bonds, the San Francisco Giants' slugger who is known for his own prodigious workouts in the baseball off–season, told *Outside* magazine, "He's unreal. He just works harder than anyone else."

Barry Bonds works hard to remain baseball's most-feared hitter.

Let me define unreal. Rice works out in the off–season six days a week: two hours of cardiovascular work in the mornings and three hours of strength training in the afternoons. His cardiovascular work consists of distance runs punctuated with a series of ten 40–meter sprints uphill. Later in the off–season he drops the uphill sprints and instead does this speed work: 6×100 meters, 6×80, 6×60, 6×40, 6×20, and 6×10. He doesn't rest between sprints and takes only two and a half minutes between sets.

For his strength work, he alternates between upper and lower body, but his workout volume remains the same: three sets of ten repetitions of twenty–one different exercises. That's 630 repetitions every day.

Rice has pioneered methods of isometric training used today by other NFL players. His training regimen is copied by other stars, though none have used it to do what Rice has done on the field. Truth be known, few if any can do what Rice does *off* the field in his training regimen. That dedication to training and conditioning helped Rice start all sixteen games for nine seasons in a row—a significant feat in a sport riddled with injuries, and with wide receivers often so susceptible to hard hits.

"I've been a workaholic over the years and I've always pushed my body to the limit," Rice told the Associated Press. "My approach has been to go out and be aggressive. It's all about preparation."

Jerry Rice's workouts are legendary, and have kept him in the game long past normal retirement age.

HEALTH: THE BOTTOM LINE

All that preparation has helped Jerry Rice not only to be the most prolific receiver in NFL history but to remain healthy and fit.

There are few things in life as important as your health.

Think about it: you could be rich, you could live in a mansion, you could have your dreams come true—but if you don't have your health, how are you going to enjoy those things? For most people, the bottom line is their health. Those who *aren't* healthy want to regain their health; it becomes the most important goal, their dearest hope in life, because their health affects all that they do.

Yet health is easy to take for granted, especially for teens. Many teens enjoy generally good health and assume they will their whole lives. If you are among that group who takes their health for granted, I have news for you: health *isn't* a given. It is directly affected by your heredity, which you can't control, and your lifestyle, which you can. It lays the foundation for you to fully enjoy and achieve all you can in sports and in all of life.

You make daily choices about your health: what you eat and drink, how active you are, what activities you take part in, how you manage stress, how you take care of your body and your mind. You might not give these choices a second thought, because they've become habitual for you—but that doesn't lessen the impact they have on your health. These daily decisions and habits you have formed, whether good habits or bad, affect you now, and they can have an increasing impact on you as you get older.

The real bottom line about health is not just that it is important, but that you can do something about achieving and maintaining it. It's your choice, and the choices you make can at times literally be life-and-death.

In this chapter I'm going to explore issues integral to health, nutrition, and fitness. These issues affect athletic performance and your quality of life. I'll also consider the challenges you face in maintaining health and fitness, and the principles that will help you be healthy and fit now and in your future.

Lynn Swann: Leading the Charge to Fitness

It's been more than twenty years since Lynn Swann, the Hall of Fame wide receiver for the Pittsburgh Steelers, graced a football field and bedazzled the crowd with his speed and acrobatic leaping ability. Swann, who played for nine years for the Steelers and who has been an ABC sportscaster for twenty-five years, looks as fit at fifty as he did at twenty-five. He has kept in shape over the years, and he has been charged by President Bush with helping to motivate Americans to increase personal fitness and become healthier. In 2003, Bush named Swann, who still does three hundred sit-ups in a given workout, chairman of the President's Council on Physical Fitness in Sports. As chairman of the council, he stresses that people find an exercise program that they enjoy and will stick with.

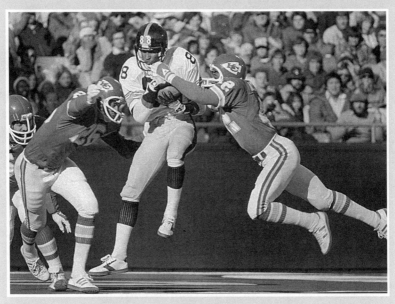

Lynn Swann, one of the most graceful wide receivers ever, remains fit, trim, and active today.

Weighty Issues

There are several issues to consider here. We'll consider three: obesity, ideal weight, and gaining and losing weight.

· · · · · · · ·

Obesity. If you're an active athlete, your chances of being obese are much less than the average American's. Being obese or over-weight is a significant problem in our country, though: more than 80 million Americans are obese, which is defined as more than 20 percent fat for men and more than 30 percent fat for women. By these standards, about one out of every three adults in America is obese.

• More than 80 million Americans—one out of every three adults—are obese.

Ideal weight. Want to know what your ideal weight is? You have to do a little math. For males, it's this: 106 pounds for 5 feet plus 6 pounds for each additional inch. So, if you're 6 feet tall, your ideal weight is 178 pounds (106 plus 72; the 72 came from 6 pounds times 12 inches). For females, it's 100 pounds for 5 feet plus 5 pounds for every additional inch. So, if you're 5 feet, 8 inches tall, your ideal weight is 140 pounds (100 plus 40; the 40 is derived from 5 pounds times 8 inches).

Gaining and losing weight. The essentials to gaining and losing weight are simple: if you take in more calories than you burn, you gain weight. If you take in fewer calories than you burn, you lose weight. Of course, the more active you are, and the higher your metabolic rate, the more calories you burn.

So what if you want to gain weight, to help you compete in a sport, to gain strength for football or for throwing the discus or for more rebounding power in basketball? You have to modify three things: your exercise, your diet, and your behavior.

To gain weight, you should be on a strength–training program to build lean body weight, and you should try to reduce calorie–burning activities. You need to take in extra calories—about 750 on strength–training days and 250 on nontraining days. Most of these extra calories should be from low–fat, protein–rich foods such as lean meats, fish, and low–fat dairy products. Finally, you need to have a weight–gain goal and reward yourself as you make progress toward that goal.

To lose weight, you need to take in fewer calories and expend more—that is, be more active. Don't go on fad diets, which can result in temporary weight loss and can be very unhealthy for you. As soon as you go off the diet, the weight comes right back. Instead, follow the guidelines I'll lay out for you in the nutrition section later in this chapter, eating a well–balanced diet that meets your body's needs, and increase your exercise. Set reasonable goals that don't call on you to lose ten pounds in two weeks; one to two pounds a week is more appropriate—and you are more likely to keep the weight off when you lose it at this rate.

> Adopt healthy eating habits now. As you age, your metabolism slows, and the tendency is to put on weight. At the same time, don't gauge your goals based on unrealistic role models—many girls want to be unhealthily thin. Strive to maintain the weight that's best for you, the weight at which you feel best.

Female Athlete Triad

The benefits of participating in sports for girls has been well cataloged: improved self-esteem, muscle strength, flexibility, and bone density; better academic achievement; lower risk for heart disease, diabetes, and stroke; and improved energy levels. (These benefits are enjoyed by boys as well.) In fact, 80 percent of women who have been identified as leaders in Fortune 500 companies participated in sports when they were younger, and a study done by the National Collegiate Athletic Association found that female student–athletes graduated at a significantly higher rate than did nonathletes. And being active in sports helps girls from becoming overweight or obese.

But there are some downsides for girls as well, some issues to be aware of. Three issues make up what is known as the "female athlete triad": disordered eating, low bone density, and amenorrhea.

- 80 percent of women who have been identified as leaders in Fortune 500 companies participated in sports when they were younger.

Disordered eating. Christy Henrich was an American gymnast who narrowly missed making the Olympic trials in 1988. After the competition in which she just missed making the cut, a judge advised her to lose some weight to improve her scores. Six years later, Henrich had starved herself to death; the four–foot–ten gymnast weighed only fifty pounds when she died of anorexia.

Anorexia is a serious psychological problem and one of the eating disorders that tends to affect females more than males (though eating disorders can affect males as well). With anorexia, people deprive their bodies of the calories and nutrients they need, going on starvation diets to lose weight. Eventually the body's organs can malfunction and shut down through extended and severe anorexia. Girls who suffer from this disorder deprive themselves of the calcium and iron they need, meaning their chances for optimal bone density are lower and their risk of stress and other fractures are higher.

Bulimia is another eating disorder. Bulimics binge and purge—meaning they eat and then force themselves to throw up, or use laxatives or diuretics to lose weight. Bulimia can lead to electrolyte imbalance and lack of essential nutrients and can cause fainting, loss of muscle, weakness, and a variety of heart problems. Like anorexia, bulimia can also cause death.

Signs of disordered eating include rapid weight loss, the desire to always eat alone, skipping meals, shying away from eating in public, being secretive around mealtime, and self-induced vomiting. People who suffer from disordered eating need immediate professional attention.

Low bone density. Female athletes incur injuries at a rate three to five times greater than their male counterparts—in part due to low bone density (also called osteoporosis). Females most susceptible to this include those in endurance sports (such as cross-country and track and field), those who compete in "aesthetic" sports (such as gymnastics and figure skating), and those who are trying to lose weight. Without proper nutrition, female athletes can incur stress fractures, which are inflammation and weakening of the outer surface of the bone.

Amenorrhea. The third part of the female athlete triad is *amenorrhea*, which is lack of menstrual periods. Primary amenorrhea occurs when menstrual periods do not begin with other signs of puberty (typically they should start by the age of sixteen). Secondary amenorrhea is when a girl misses three or more consecutive periods after she has begun menstruating.

Both types of amenorrhea are fairly common among female athletes. The risk is that either type can lead to abnormally low bone density. This can affect female athletes both now (through stress fractures and other bone problems) and later (through osteoporosis). To combat amenorrhea, girls need to increase their caloric intake and make sure they get enough sleep and proper nutrition.

> These three issues are of critical importance to females. If you are having problems with any of these issues—especially with disordered eating—or know someone who is, seek help immediately.

Smoking

An estimated 440,000 Americans die each year from diseases caused by smoking. Lung disease is America's number three killer, responsible for one in seven deaths. Further, more than 25 million Americans suffer from chronic lung disease.

Every day, six thousand kids under age eighteen smoke their first cigarette. Of these, three thousand will become regular smokers. That amounts to 2 million new smokers annually—and they're teens or younger.

The tobacco industry spends billions of dollars per year to lure new smokers. Advertisements make you think it's cool and fun to smoke, it brings zest to your life, it makes you more attractive, more free, more independent. The reality is it shortens your life, makes you more miserable while you live it, and enslaves you to a filthy and expensive habit.

Yet one recent national survey showed that 28 percent of high schoolers currently smoked cigarettes. (Not surprisingly, smoking is more prevalent among those who don't make it past their junior year in high school—35.4 percent—than those who have a college degree—11.6 percent.)

> • Every day, six thousand kids under age eighteen smoke their first cigarette. Of these, three thousand will become regular smokers.

Smoking is cool? Yeah, if you like to expose yourself to an array of serious and life-threatening respiratory illnesses, if you don't mind limiting your lung function, if you don't mind dying prematurely. Then it's *way* cool.

National studies also link tobacco use with these "cool" behaviors: being involved in fights, carrying weapons, engaging in high-risk sexual behavior, and using alcohol and other drugs.

Use your head and be kind to your heart. The most telling of all statistics about smoking is this: Every death caused by smoking is preventable.

The message is simple: If you want to get the most out of your life as an athlete and as a person, don't smoke. If you *do* smoke, seek professional help to quit.

Nancy Lopez: Stroking Against Strokes

Nancy Lopez, an LPGA Hall of Fame golfer, annually plays against other golfers to raise money to help the American Stroke Association in its mission of reducing death and disability from stroke. An estimated 97,000 women die from stroke each year in the United States.

Lopez, whose mother died from a heart attack in 1978 and whose father has survived a heart attack, has an increased risk of stroke and heart disease because of her family history. To reduce her risk for cardiovascular disease, she adheres to a strict exercise regimen and a healthy diet.

Alcohol and Other Drugs

According to films, television shows, and much of what you see in the print media, alcohol has much the same effect as cigarettes: it makes life fun, it makes you cool, it makes you attractive to the opposite sex. All of which is a sham.

Alcohol is especially appealing to kids who are trying to fit in, to be accepted. And it's readily available and commonly used. In fact, alcohol is the number one drug of choice for teens in the United States. By their senior year in high school, 80 percent of teens have tried alcohol, compared with 47 percent who have tried marijuana and 29 percent who have tried another illegal drug. More than 5 million high school students admit to binge drinking at least once a month, according to a national study done in 2002 by Columbia University researchers.

And it's not just in the high schools; there's an epidemic of underage drinking in elementary and middle schools. For the class of 1975, 27 percent of the high school graduating class began using alcohol in eighth grade or earlier. In 1999, that number had risen to 36 percent. Consumption is fairly equal between boys and girls.

Some people use alcohol as a form of self-medication. It makes them feel better about their world, at least for a short time. It lets them escape their worries and troubles. It appeals especially to teens who have low self-esteem, anxiety, and depression. It's seen as a quick fix.

- Alcohol is the number one drug of choice for teens. By their senior year in high school, 80 percent of teens have tried alcohol, compared with 47 percent who have tried marijuana and 29 percent who have tried another illegal drug.

But it doesn't fix anything. It doesn't make them cool, more attractive to the opposite sex, or more likely to be accepted by the "in" crowd.

If it doesn't do any of the things it is purported to do, what *does* it do? For one thing, it leads to a huge increase in unprotected sex. Teens who drink are seven times more likely to engage in sex and twice as likely to have sex with multiple partners than those who do not.

Unprotected sex brings with it the increased risk of AIDS, of other sexually transmitted diseases—and 15 million new cases of sexually transmitted diseases occur each year in the United States—and of becoming pregnant. About 70 percent of college students admit to having engaged in sexual activity *primarily because they were drunk* and said they wouldn't have had sex if they had been sober. It affects college students in another way as well: Nearly 159,000 of today's first-year college students will drop out of school next year for alcohol- or drug-related reasons.

- There are more than 15 million new cases of sexually transmitted diseases each year in the United States.

Alcohol poses the greatest threat to teens' well-being, because it impairs judgment and leads to driving while intoxicated, engaging in risky sexual behavior, and trying other drugs. It is a contributing factor in the top three causes of death among teens: accidents, homicide, and suicide. It poisons bodies and damages brains, hearts, and livers. It is highly addictive.

Other drugs. As for other drugs, teen use of cocaine is on the rise: 9.4 percent reported using it at least once in their life, whereas in 1991 only 5.9 percent reported using it at least once. About 9 percent of teens use the drug Ecstasy. In 1994, there were 253 emergency room episodes related to Ecstasy; in 2001, that number leaped to 5,542.

Annual illicit drug use by high school seniors peaked at 54 percent in 1979, dipped to a low of 27 percent in 1992, but then rose again to 42 percent in the late 1990s. As with alcohol, illicit drugs are addictive and can cause a variety of problems to mental and physical health.

Steroids. Anabolic and androgenic steroids are man-made substances related to male sex hormones. They help build muscle and they increase masculine characteristics. They are especially attractive to athletes who want to gain strength and enhance their performance. Many people also take them in an effort to improve their physical appearance.

Teen steroid use rose steadily in the 1990s; in 1999, 3 percent of teens reported that they had taken anabolic steroids at least once. Anabolic steroids can cause permanent damage to the heart, liver, and kidneys and has a host of other unhealthy physical and psychiatric effects. For men, it causes shrinking of the testicles, reduced sperm count, infertility, baldness, development of breasts, and an increased risk for prostate cancer. For women, it causes growth of facial hair, male-pattern baldness, changes in or stopping of the menstrual cycle, enlargement of the clitoris, and a deepened voice.

For adolescents, it halts growth prematurely if they take steroids before they have experienced their final growth spurts.

While most anabolic steroid users are male, in 1998 it was reported that about 175,000 high school girls used illegal anabolic steroids, double the number of girls that had used the drugs in 1991.

Steroids are an illegal shortcut to athletic success, and not necessarily an effective shortcut at that. Regardless of their effectiveness in enhancing athletic performance, the serious and permanent side effects should be enough to keep athletes from resorting to this illegal and dangerous method to enhance their performance.

The message with smoking, alcohol, and other drugs is clear: Keep your body clean, your mind clear and focused. Smoking and drugs don't make you cool, smart, attractive, or accepted. They harm and can eventually destroy your body and, in some cases, your mind. If you smoke or drink or use other drugs because you are anxious or depressed, then seek help for that anxiety or depression, because you're not going to find help in a pack of cigarettes, a six-pack of beer, or a line of cocaine. If you use any of these substances because you have low self-esteem, because you want to be accepted by others, because you are following the crowd, take a closer look at yourself. Do you really need friends like that? Do you really need their "approval"? You're worth more than that. If you use these substances, your self-esteem will spiral even lower. Don't be afraid to take a closer look at who you really are and what talents and gifts you possess. Focus on what you have, not on what you don't have, and concentrate on building up what you have. You can't possibly reach your potential, athletically or otherwise, if you abuse your body and your mind. Make your own choices and decisions—and make them healthy ones.

Drugs destroy countless thousands of people's lives every year. They cause permanent damage, they cause violence and crime, they kill. They land people in jail, they result in lost jobs, ruined reputations, and bleak futures. Don't allow yourself to become one more drug statistic.

Lyle Alzado: Brought Down by Steroids

Lyle Alzado was an All-Pro defensive lineman in the NFL in the 1970s and 1980s, playing for the Denver Broncos, Cleveland Browns, and Los Angeles Raiders. After his career was over he admitted that he began using steroids in college and never stopped throughout the rest of his career. He talked about how addictive steroids were and how violent they made him, not only on the field but off.

He also said his last wish was that no one else die the way he did: weak, wracked with pain, unable to walk on his own, unable to remember things. Lyle Alzado died at age forty-three of brain cancer brought on by excessive steroid use.

Lyle Alzado's final wish: that athletes stay away from steroids.

Other Health Issues

There are a variety of other health issues that affect you. I'm going to talk about three of them: stress management, injuries, and sleep.

Stress management. People talk about "good stress" and "bad stress" (or distress). When the game is on the line, that's stressful—and some athletes handle it better than others. When you have a big test to study for, that can be stressful. Again, some rise to the occasion while others shrink from it.

Relationships with family and with friends—and with coaches and teachers—can be stressful. There are numerous other issues that can cause stress: your parents get divorced, someone close to you dies, you break up with your girlfriend or boyfriend, you're having problems in your classes, you just moved to a new city or new school, you just lost your starting spot on the team, and on and on. Stress is a part of life, and you have to learn how to recognize stressful situations and how to respond to them in a healthy manner.

How do you know if you're stressed out? Stress shows in a variety of ways: You get sick more often. You feel anxious or depressed or panicky. You are more irritable and cause more accidents to happen. You get in trouble at school or with your coach or parents because you act out. You smoke or use alcohol or drugs. You lose interest in school or in sports and in your own achievements. You withdraw from family and friends. You have suicidal thoughts.

Of course, no one is going to have all these signs of stress, but if you experience one or more of them, recognize them for what they are and share your feelings and concerns with your parents and with those you trust. Identify the problems and then map out behaviors, attitudes, and plans that will help you alleviate the problems before they become too big.

Injuries. Injuries, like stress, are a part of life, especially for athletes. Injuries can range from minor to serious, can occur at one time (acute injury) or over a long period of time (overuse injury). They can happen because of extrinsic factors (training load too heavy, strained muscles from cold weather, playing field in poor condition) or intrinsic factors (muscle imbalance, lack of training, previous injury).

To avoid injuries, and to recover from them as quickly as possible when you are injured, respect what your body is telling you. Talk to your coach if you feel you are injured, rather than just playing through it. Take the time to heal, and fulfill your responsibility in bringing about the healing—for example, if you have a sprained ankle, make sure you ice the ankle, keep it elevated, take ibuprofen or another anti-inflammatory to reduce the inflammation, and keep the ankle compressed with supportive wrapping or tape to prevent further injury.

Sleep. To refuel our bodies and our minds, we need sleep. Teens need at least eight hours of sleep each night, and athletes often need more than that, because the demands they place on their bodies are greater.

> The first steps to handling stress are to acknowledge it and talk about it with someone else.

NUTRITION: ENERGY TO BURN

If sleep refuels our bodies, nutrition fuels them. Good nutrition is a foundation to health and to athletic performance; without it, your engine is going to sputter and run out of gas. In this section I'll help you consider what good nutrition is—that is, what you need to fuel your body—and I'll take a look at some special needs and considerations for athletes as well.

Fuel for Your Engine

What are your nutritional needs as an athlete? Your daily diet should consist of the following:

- two to three servings of lean meat, poultry, fish, dry beans, eggs (one serving is three ounces)
- three to four servings of milk, yogurt, cheese (one serving is one cup of milk)
- six to eleven servings of breads, cereals, pastas, rice (one serving is one slice of bread or one-half cup of pasta, rice, or cereal)
- three to five servings of vegetables (one serving is one-half cup cooked or one cup raw)
- two to four servings of fruit (one serving is one medium piece of fruit)

As an athlete your calorie intake should be about 60 to 70 percent carbohydrates, about 15 percent protein, and the remainder (15 to 25 percent) fat. Let's take a brief look at the individual nutrients your body needs to function optimally, to stay healthy, and to perform at your maximum in sports.

Carbohydrates. You need more carbohydrates because they fuel your muscles during exercise, they are your greatest source of energy, and your body stores them in limited amounts. After a hard practice or game, you should replenish your carbohydrates within an hour, if possible, for most efficient storage.

Foods high in carbohydrates include bread, bagels, pasta, rice, potatoes, waffles, fruit juices, and many vegetables and fruits.

Protein. More is not always better. Although muscles are made up primarily of protein, eating an excess amount of protein can actually hamper performance—and eating extra protein doesn't increase your muscle size. Extra protein is burned up for energy or stored as fat.

As a general guide, sedentary teens need about 1 gram of protein per kilogram of body weight. Active teenage athletes need about 1.2 to 1.5 grams per kilogram of weight. (A kilogram is about 0.45 of one pound.) Check out the following figures to see some examples of how much protein teen athletes should consume. .

- 130 pounds = 58.5 kilograms = 70 to 88 grams of protein per day
- 150 pounds = 67.5 kilograms = 81 to 101 grams of protein per day
- 170 pounds = 76.5 kilograms = 92 to 115 grams of protein per day
- 190 pounds = 85.5 kilograms = 102 to 128 grams of protein per day

So what's a gram? Here are gram contents of protein in various foods:

- cheeseburger (4–ounce patty): 30 grams of protein
- lean meat, fish, poultry (3–ounce serving): 22 grams
- cheese pizza (one slice): 15 grams
- taco: 9 grams
- milk (from skim to whole, 8 ounces): 8 grams
- low–fat yogurt: 8 grams
- bagel: 7 grams
- peanut butter (1 tablespoon): 5 grams
- whole wheat bread (one slice): 3 grams

Fat. Our bodies need fat, but the average American diet contains much more fat than we need. Fats make foods taste good, but excess fat—especially highly saturated fat—can increase the risk of heart disease. Watch your fat intake, especially at fast-food restaurants. A little later I'll give you a few tips about eating healthily at fast-food restaurants.

Vitamins and minerals. Vitamins and minerals are important for food metabolism and for converting food to energy. Vitamin B_6

helps absorb protein and aids in carbohydrate metabolism; Vitamin D helps build and maintain bones; iron helps muscular endurance and is especially vital for girls; calcium builds bones and teeth and promotes nerve and cell function; and on and on. By eating a good diet, you should be able to get all the vitamins and minerals you need without using supplements.

Fluids and electrolytes. Fluid needs are critical to both health and athletic performance. If you wait until you're thirsty to drink, you've waited too long—and in the case of athletic performance, you've diminished your capabilities. You require about eight cups of fluid per day—much more if you're an athlete. A 150-pound athlete can lose as much as six cups of fluid in one hour of exercise. For every pound of weight you lose during a work-out, you should drink two cups of fluid to replace it. Water, juices, and sport drinks are good fluids to drink—though realize that sport drinks are designed for exercise that lasts longer than sixty minutes.

- A 150-pound athlete can lose as much as six cups of fluid in one hour of exercise. For every pound of weight you lose during a workout, you should drink two cups of fluid to replace it.

Healthy snacks. Snacks are an important part of a healthy diet, especially for athletes, who burn many more calories than seden-tary people. Sandwiches, juice boxes, energy bars, fruits, pretzels, crackers, and similar foods are healthy, easily digested, and pro-vide you with carbohydrates to quickly convert to energy. Just make sure you focus most of your snacking on foods high in car-bohydrates, not in fat.

If you want your body to be a fine-tuned engine, you better be putting premium-performance fuel in it. Follow sound nutritional guidelines and stay away from fad diets.

Special Considerations

In addition to those dietary needs, athletes have some special issues to consider as well, including pregame meals and eating on the road.

Pregame meals. You should eat a meal high in carbohydrates about two to three hours before a game. Doing so will give you the maximum energy you need to compete. Make sure you drink at least two cups of water a few hours before the game, and drink about a half cup every fifteen minutes or so during the game or during a workout.

Eating on the road. Getting good nutrition on the road is tricky, because most of the offerings in restaurants—especially fast-food restaurants—are high in fat. Whether you're eating before or after a game, you don't want a high-fat meal; you want a high-carbohydrate meal.

So what do you do when your team bus pulls into the parking lot of a fast-food restaurant? Here are a few tips.

- Choose low-fat or fat-free milk instead of soda. Through the milk you get vitamin D, calcium, and protein; through the soda you get only sugar or artificial sweetener.
- Bring along your own fruits or vegetables: an apple, an orange, or a banana; tomato juice, some baby carrots, some broccoli or cauliflower. All of these travel well.
- Avoid foods high in sugar, fat, and sodium—in other words, the majority of the menu! Choose chicken rather than beef, because chicken has less fat. And choose it broiled—not breaded and fried.
- In general, steer clear of pizza, hot dogs, and French fries—or anything fried. These foods are all high in fat and sodium.
- Hit the salad bar! But when you do, hit it with eyes wide open, because lots of the choices there are high in fat, too: pasta salads, potato salads, salad dressings. The best advice here is to go

for lettuce and spinach salads with vegetables. The deeper green a vegetable is, the more vitamins it contains (so, romaine lettuce and spinach are more nutritious for you than the pale green iceberg lettuce). Choose fruit salads also.

CHALLENGES TO A HEALTHY AND FIT LIFESTYLE

A healthy lifestyle is one in which you make conscious choices that benefit your body and your mind, that steer you toward a life in which you feel vibrant and strong and in which you take care of yourself. Issues involved here include what I've talked about so far: eating healthily, getting enough sleep, managing your stress, and staying away from smoking, alcohol and other drugs, and from harmful behaviors.

A fit lifestyle is one in which you hone your body and your physical talents. Fitness has to do with endurance, speed, strength, and other factors, which I'll explore in the next chapter. Lots of people are healthy and live healthy lifestyles; the best athletes are those who are healthy *and* fit.

While it might seem, at your age, that health and fitness are natural things, and that you'll always have them, this isn't necessarily the case. The battle to retain health and fitness gets harder with age, and even at your age there are many issues that can act as roadblocks to your own health and fitness. You need to understand what those issues are and how they can affect you. Here are a few of those issues.

Heredity. You can't change your parents no matter how much you at times might wish you could! You inherit a lot from them—including tendencies to be thin or overweight, to have high or low risk for heart disease, cancer, and other disease, and a host of other factors that affect your health and fitness levels. You can't change your heredity, but you can change your lifestyle.

Lifestyle. We've talked about lifestyle already—the daily choices you make affect your health and your fitness and define your lifestyle. It's easy to not think about the choices after a while, and this can be dangerous, because you can ingrain unhealthy choices into your daily pattern, and these choices affect your academic and social life and your athletic performance. So you need to reexamine your lifestyle choices, look at them anew as if you've never made the choices before, and make sure that the decisions you make are ones that benefit you and help you build toward a bright future.

Lack of knowledge. Sometimes we make poor choices because we simply don't know better. That used to be the case with people who smoked cigarettes; long ago people weren't aware of the health risks that came with cigarette smoking (though that's no longer the case). The point is to arm yourself with information that can help you make good decisions. For instance, don't just take steroids because you think they will improve your performance. Find out the consequences of taking steroids, what they do to your body and your mind. Once you find that out, you'd be foolish to take them. Don't use "I didn't know" as an excuse; find out what you need to know and then make responsible decisions.

Beliefs and attitudes. During the Great Depression, which began in 1929, the more overweight a person was, the more prosperous and well-off that person was believed to be. The thinking went that overweight people had enough money to eat well. That may have been partially true, but being overweight has never been healthy. What you believe regarding health and fitness, and what your attitudes are, based on your beliefs, go a long way toward shaping your behavior.

If you believe that hard work and dedication are going to result in your athletic improvement and in your coach playing you more, then you'll work harder and be more committed. If you feel that no matter what you do, your coach isn't going to notice you, then you will be tempted to slack off and not care.

Similarly, if you believe that no matter what you do, you're not going to be very healthy or fit, then you'll probably make some poor decisions. Your beliefs and attitudes greatly affect how you approach life.

Difficulty in changing behavior. Donnell started smoking cigarettes when he was thirteen because he thought smoking was cool. Now he's sixteen and he's serious about track and field—he's a middle distance runner. Smoking, of course, is not only bad for Donnell's health; it seriously affects his fitness level, because it cuts the amount of oxygen his blood can carry. He loves track and wants to excel, but, incredibly, he finds he can't cut out the smoking, because he's addicted.

Changing behavior is often very difficult, whether you're trying to break an addiction or you're simply trying to change your study habits or your diet. Patterns become ingrained in us and sometimes even highly motivated people have difficulty changing behavior. Often this difficulty lies in wanting immediate and complete change and not being prepared for a struggle. Change typically happens over time, in small steps, and with some missteps along the way. "Two steps forward, one step backward" is not an entirely bad way to go, so long as the general progression keeps moving forward. Change takes motivation and desire, a well-thought-out plan, accountability to someone else who can provide support, and commitment.

At times—especially in terms of addiction or use of nicotine, alcohol, or other drugs—change is aided by professionals who know how to help you drop harmful habits and adopt healthy ones. In a case like this, asking for help is not a sign of weakness; it is a sign of maturity.

Peer pressure. Depending on who you hang out with, you might feel pressure to train hard and do well in school, or you might feel pressure to drink, to use drugs, or to engage in other unhealthy (and unlawful) behaviors. How you respond to that pressure is entirely up to you. The pull of peer pressure can be powerful and strong, like the pull of a swift and mighty river. Don't get swept up in a current that takes you in the wrong direction. Weigh your decisions based on what's best for you.

Lack of training. How well you train, of course, affects your health to some extent and certainly your fitness for athletic performance. How you train, how focused and dedicated you are in your pursuit of athletic excellence, is up to you. Coasting has its consequences, one of them being that no matter how good you are, your competition will catch up to you if you don't focus on your own training and improving your performance. If you're not very dedicated to your sports training right now, it's highly unlikely that you'll be very committed to living a healthy and fit lifestyle later on in life.

> If you recognize the challenges you face in attaining and maintaining optimal health and fitness, you're way ahead of the game, because most people don't give these very serious issues a second thought.

LIVING THE HEALTHY AND FIT LIFE

So how do you live the healthy and fit life? I see six keys to doing so.

1. Assess where you are now.
The first thing you need to do is assess your current status. How healthy and fit are you right now? How do your levels of health and fitness affect your life and your athletic performance? What areas could you stand to improve in? What areas do you excel in? Before you make plans to change, you have to know your strengths and weaknesses—what you want to change, what you want to build upon.

2. Understand where you need to go.

Once you assess your strengths and weaknesses, you begin to form an idea of where you need to go from here to improve your overall health and fitness. Maybe you need to make improvements in your diet; maybe you need to get to sleep an hour earlier; maybe you need to work harder in the off-season. An honest assessment (and don't be afraid to ask your coach or parents or anyone else who is in a position to help you assess yourself) helps you begin to form the plans to make improvements in your life.

3. Know the challenges you face.

We just talked about many of the challenges you face in living a healthy and fit lifestyle. Which challenges are most apparent in your life? What are your biggest roadblocks to health and fitness? Why are these roadblocks for you? Knowing your challenges is crucial, because no matter how motivated you are in attaining health and fitness, if you don't understand the challenges, you can keep running into the same roadblocks without getting around them.

4. Set goals.

Setting goals helps you map out your course of action to get around those roadblocks. Once you know the challenges you face, how can you best get around them? Remember to set meaningful, realistic, and well-defined goals, ones that challenge you but that are reachable, and ones that provide checkpoints along the way.

5. Work toward goals with the help of others.

If one of your goals is to work out harder in the off-season, recruit a teammate or friend to work out with you. It's harder to break a commitment if it involves someone else. Tell others about your health and fitness goals, and be accountable to them—tell them how you're doing. In many cases other people can offer not only support and encouragement but sound advice in helping you stay on track to reach your goals.

6. Stay committed for the long haul.

Health and fitness are lifelong commitments. Adopt healthy habits and make sure that you maintain them throughout this year, throughout high school and college, and throughout life. Being healthy and fit bring with them great side benefits, including feeling better and more energetic, being more productive in whatever you do, and enjoying life to its fullest extent.

Valerie Brisco: Golden Goals

In 1982, not long after giving birth to her son, Valerie Brisco was forty pounds overweight and had no plans to return to track and field, a sport in which she had excelled in college. Her husband, Alvin Hooks, then a wide receiver for the Philadelphia Eagles, talked her into getting back into shape and returning to the sport she loved.

She got back into shape with a vengeance. Her training and dedication were rewarded with three gold medals in the 1984 Olympics, where she became the first woman since Wilma Rudolph in 1960 to win three gold medals in one Olympiad. Brisco, who captured her gold medals in the 200 and 400 meters and in the 4×400-meter relay, set Olympic and American records in the two individual events and became the first person, male or female, to win the 200 and 400 (in 21.81 and 48.83, respectively) in the same Olympics. She was also the first American woman to dip under 50 seconds in the 400.

> There's no hocus-pocus involved in being healthy and fit—just under-standing and wisdom, with some perseverance and commitment sprinkled in.

Much of that enjoyment for you right now comes from your athletic endeavors. How much you enjoy your sports experience depends in great part on how you perform. In the next chapter I'll take a look at how you can improve your athletic performance.

7

IMPROVE YOUR ATHLETIC PERFORMANCE

DAVE WINFIELD: AT THE TOP OF HIS GAME

At the age of fifty-one, San Diego Padres vice president Dave Winfield exchanged his business suit for more familiar togs—a baseball uniform with his old No. 31 on it. He spent time in the Padres' 2003 spring training camp as a guest instructor, and the seven-time Gold Glover flashed the leather as he demonstrated his ability to charge balls in the outfield and go into his accurate, over-the-top throwing motion that nailed, over his twenty-two-year career, 166 base runners.

Winfield hadn't lost much in speed, quickness, or agility. The Padres players were riveted to his performance and his words, because they knew Winfield had been there, done that. And all that he had done (see the box below) landed him in the Hall of Fame—one of only nine players to make it without playing a day in the minor leagues.

Dave Winfield Highlights

Batting average: .283

Home runs: 465

Runs batted in: 1,833

Hits: 3,110

Ranks in the Top 20 all-time in hits, runs batted in, games, at-bats, doubles, and total bases

One of seven players to reach 3,000 hits and 400 home runs

12 consecutive All-Star appearances

7 Gold Gloves

Elected to Hall of Fame in 2001

Winfield went straight from the University of Minnesota to the Padres. By signing with the Padres, he turned down potential contracts with the Atlanta Hawks of the NBA (Winfield starred in basketball as well as baseball at Minnesota), the Utah Stars of the ABA, and the Minnesota Vikings of the NFL. Winfield is the only athlete to be drafted by professional teams in three sports.

Winfield knew how to get the most out of his abilities and how to continually improve his performance. For example, he had one of the most productive seasons ever for a forty–year–old when he hit .290 with 26 home runs and 108 runs batted in for the Toronto Blue Jays in 1992. Only four other players had both more hits and more home runs than Winfield: Hank Aaron, Willie Mays, Eddie Murray, and Stan Musial.

And he performed in the spotlight: he played nine seasons with the New York Yankees, under the fiery and sometimes harsh leadership of Yankees owner George Steinbrenner. When Steinbrenner chided Winfield for not being able to "hit for average," Winfield shortened his home–run stroke in 1984 and battled teammate Don Mattingly for the American League batting crown (Mattingly ended up winning the crown, hitting .343 to Winfield's .340).

Steinbrenner had little to complain about, because Winfield was the first Yankee since the legendary Joe DiMaggio to drive in over a hundred runs in five consecutive seasons.

Winfield didn't restrict his achievements to the baseball diamond. In 1994 he received the Roberto Clemente Man of the Year Award, given to the player who best exemplifies baseball on and off the field. Long before that he had established the David M. Winfield

Dave Winfield's efforts were rewarded by being inducted in 2001 into baseball's Hall of Fame.

Foundation, which provides free baseball tickets and health examinations to underprivileged children. He is a member of numerous boards and is a bestselling author, respected motivational speaker, and corporate spokesman.

Among Winfield's topics as a motivational speaker are many of the topics in this book: setting goals, assessing values, achieving success, having a vision, overcoming adversity, fulfilling dreams, thinking outside the box, and eliminating negativity.

Because Winfield excels in all those areas, he performed at the top of his game on the field—and he continues to excel off the field.

KEEP IN SHAPE YEAR-ROUND

Dave Winfield excelled in baseball because he kept himself ready to perform. If you want to get the most out of your abilities, you have to stay in shape year-round. Your training should have variety so that you don't get bored, and it should include some downtime to rest and recuperate immediately following your competitive season. Other than that downtime, which should last one or two weeks, you should be active throughout the rest of the year.

And not just active for the sake of being physically fit, but active with a plan in mind: to improve your abilities as an athlete. You need to develop a specific off-season training program, one that takes your strengths and weaknesses into account, one that is shaped to develop your physical abilities and your mental tough-ness, and to add real value to your total package as an athlete.

I'm not going to lay out specific training programs for you, because your program will depend on your sport, your abilities, and your needs, but I'll define program components that are commonly used. I encourage you to talk to your school trainer, if you have one, or your coach, to set up your training program.

One way to structure your year-round training is in three phases: preparation, competition, and transition.

Preparation Phase

This is the longest phase. If you play one sport, the preparation phase lasts about five or six months (leading up to a four- to five-month season and about a one-month transition period). If you play two sports, the preparation phase is, of course, shortened, because you spend twice as much time competing. Regardless of how many sports you play, you should have a preparation phase of at least two to three months each year.

So what goes on in this phase? It's divided into two parts—first, general conditioning, followed by specific preparation for the season. In the general conditioning portion, you work on developing the highest level of conditioning, which lays the foundation for both future training and competition. Based on your sport and your performance needs, you focus your training in these general conditioning areas: strength, speed, endurance, agility, quickness, and flexibility.

In the specific preparation portion, you move from general conditioning to specific sport skills and exercises as you hone your talents. As the competitive season approaches, the volume of training drops, but the quality, intensity, and the sport-specific flavor of your workouts increase.

Competition Phase

This includes all training done with your team during your season—the preseason and in-season training and postseason competition. Here you focus on improving your ability to execute the techniques and tactics of your sport as well as improving your mental skills. The training during a season is always more exciting, because you can see your improvement from game to game as you gain competitive experience.

Transition Phase

This phase allows your body to recuperate from the rigors of training for many months on end and from a competitive and exhausting season of games and practices. The object here is to relax, to heal any minor aches and pains or injuries that have cropped up, and to refresh both your mind and body.

During this phase, which lasts about a month, you might take a week entirely off and then begin light activity and training—nothing strenuous, about half the load of normal training, or even less.

Why remain active during this phase? Because through inactivity you quickly lose much of what you worked to attain throughout the rest of the year. You lose 3 to 4 percent of your strength in a week that you take off, and those losses increase if you remain inactive. The same type of loss occurs with speed, agility, and endurance. This is the "use it or lose it" principle of training that all athletes—no matter how talented—are subjected to.

Off-Season Training

The off-season training—the preparation phase—is really the most critical element here. Once you're in-season, you follow your coach's plans, but in the off-season you are responsible for arriving at the first practice in the best possible shape. Here, then, are a few pointers about shaping your off-season program.

1. Train with a plan in mind.

As I mentioned, work with your trainer or coach to devise the best off-season plan for you. Check out books on training for your sport. Find out what the best athletes are doing and adapt it to fit your own needs. Know what you need to develop and focus your plan on those elements. Map it out beforehand; don't just go down to the weight room and casually lift a few weights. Go down with a plan in mind and the specific exercises to help you develop strength, quickness, and explosive power.

2. Make it fun.

The off-season is long. If you stick to the same routine day after day, you run the risk of losing interest and slacking off on your training or dropping it altogether. Keep it fresh and varied and make it fun. A little later I'll provide a sample program that reflects variety and that can help maintain interest in off-season training.

3. Make it challenging.

Fun doesn't mean easy. You need to challenge yourself in your training. Most top athletes, in fact, equate challenging with fun—it's the challenge that keeps them going. You won't improve if you don't challenge yourself.

4. Train with a partner.

Part of making it fun is to train with a friend. When you train with a friend you tend to be more committed to your own workouts, and you can encourage each other along the way. If you can, find a training partner or two to work out with during the off-season.

5. Set goals.

I've talked about the importance of setting goals before; they're important in off-season training, too. Without goals it's easy to just drift along in your training. If you have specific goals in developing strength, speed, endurance, or any other facet of conditioning, then you have something to work toward, something to keep you going.

6. Check progress.

Set up benchmarks you want to reach for each month of training in each facet. Then you and your training partner can test yourselves along the way. It's helpful to know how you're doing, and noting improvements can fuel your motivation to further improve. (And if you're not improving, that realization can fuel your desire to step up your training.)

7. Reward yourself.

As you reach goals along the way, reward yourself in some appropriate and fun ways. Rewards break up the monotony of training and give you something to shoot for besides the improved condition.

8. Stick with it.

The off-season is long. You probably will experience some ups and downs in your training; the main point is to stick with it. Don't get discouraged and give up. In normal training, progression doesn't go up in a smooth line; it goes up, then plateaus off for a while, then you break through to a new level. Don't get fooled by the training plateaus. Ride them out, stick with your training, and you'll be rewarded in your competitive season.

Sample Program

While I am not supplying a specific training program for you, I can provide you a sample program that reflects the basics of what I've just laid out. Your general off–season program might look something like this:

- Monday: skill development, weight training (upper body), agility drills, conditioning, stretching
- Tuesday: skill development, plyometrics, weight training (lower body), stretching
- Wednesday: skill development, medicine ball work
- Thursday: skill development, weight training (upper body), agility drills, conditioning, stretching
- Friday: skill development, plyometrics, weight training (lower body), stretching

What you put into something is what you get out of it. If you aren't willing to do the work, then don't complain about not playing as much or achieving as much as you wanted to. Consistent work and a mature approach in the off-season will help you get to where you want to be in your next season.

HONE YOUR SPORT-SPECIFIC SKILLS

As you can see from that sample program, much of the off–season is devoted to honing your physical skills. That, of course, is fundamental to your development as a player—and the conditioning that goes into the off-season supports your skill development. That is, as you get stronger and faster and can last longer, your ability to execute the tactics and skills of your sport will improve. Without that buildup in the off-season, you limit your ability to improve your sport-specific skills.

I'm sure your coach has drilled it into your head that you need to learn the fundamental skills first. Professional players in all sports spend their preseasons and even their in-season practices working on refining their execution of the basic skills of their game. One truth about sports is you can *always* improve, even in your execution of the basics—otherwise why do turnovers happen in basketball and football, misplays happen in baseball, unforced errors happen in tennis, and so on?

As you gain experience and grow in expertise, you can take on the more advanced skills of your sport. But as you do so, you continue to practice the basics, because you continue to need to refine those skills, and the majority of your game is spent in executing basic skills, no matter how advanced a player you are. The all-time greats are so because they mastered the basic skills and almost flawlessly performed them game in and game out, not because they brought some exotic twist or flair to their game or learned some advanced skills that they got to use once every other game.

So my advice to you is to keep it simple, keep it basic, focus on the fundamentals, and once you show mastery of them, begin to incorporate more advanced skills. As you do, learn from the best—watch professional and collegiate players on TV or in person, purchase good skills videos and books, go to sports camps, and continually look for ways to improve and build on your own skills.

Don't be afraid to ask your coach for extra help in mastering skills. One way to improve your game is to play against slightly better opponents—playing against (or training with) someone who is vastly superior or inferior to you won't be of much use to either player. If you choose a training partner who is close to you in ability, one who is perhaps better in some aspects but maybe lacking in other aspects, you can help each other refine your skills.

The main point is never stop honing your skills—in the off-season, preseason, in-season, throughout the year. No matter how good you are, don't stop, because you're not there yet. With consistent work—and with the required mental toughness—you might one day get there, though.

> When you practice your skills, practice with a purpose. Know what you're trying to improve and use drills and exercises that focus on that particular skill you're working on.

ACHIEVE MENTAL TOUGHNESS

Michael Jordan had it in basketball. Walter Payton had it in football. Roger Clemens has it in baseball. Serena Williams, Mia Hamm, Lisa Leslie: they all have it.

Mental toughness has helped these athletes set themselves apart. It has elevated their game and, in the case of team sports, it has elevated their whole team. True mental toughness is a precious commodity in sports—and in all other pursuits.

Ichiro Suzuki: Competing—and Achieving—Against the Best

For many years, Ichiro Suzuki was one of Japan's brightest baseball stars, averaging over .350 as a hitter. Prior to the 2001 season, he signed with the Seattle Mariners because, he said, he wanted to play against the very best, to see how he could do.

He has done all right and then some. Ichiro led the American League in hitting his first year, hitting .350, stealing 56 bases, and leading the Mariners to the play-offs. He followed that with a .321 season in 2002. Ichiro also donates Mariners tickets to various organizations and is involved in the community in a number of ways.

You've seen the players who have all the physical skills yet somehow never seem to get their game together. These players haven't worked on developing their mental skills and tend to wilt in the heat of competition. No matter how good you are, you won't get far without the mental toughness it takes to be a winner in sports.

I addressed some of the mental aspects of athletic success in Chapter 1, but I'll go into more detail here. I'm going to point out eight keys that will help you achieve mental toughness—and thus help you perform to the best of your ability.

1. Adopt a winning attitude.

I've talked about attitude before, but this is worth repeating: If you don't think you can be a winner, you've sealed your fate. If you don't think you have to work hard because you have superior skills, you won't be prepared for the next level of competition and you won't do as well as you could at your current level. If you shy away from hard work or have a negative attitude, you won't get very far.

Your attitude propels everything and can make things happen that didn't seem possible. Athletes who have a winning attitude are the ones who separate themselves from their competition—even at times when their competition is more physically skilled. When you have a winning attitude, you don't know the meaning of giving up or not giving every practice and every game and every off-season workout your full effort. People with winning attitudes are the most likely to get the most out of their abilities, and to remain mentally tough when the game is on the line or when the odds are against them.

How do you adopt a winning attitude? You can't change your personality, but you can shift, little by little, how you think about things. You can be more appreciative of your present gifts and abilities, of your current situation. You can focus on the positives in your life. You can see life as a series of lessons to be learned, victories to be won. You can look to the future and not dwell in the past. You can dwell on your personal victories and achievements rather than lament your losses and mistakes.

If you're on the bench, don't moan and complain or give up. Learn all you can from the starters on the team, figure out the skills you need to improve to get more playing time, enjoy your role as a substitute helping your team win. And realize that there are tons of kids out there who aren't even on the team that would like to be.

People with winning attitudes are ones who enjoy the day and move forward with focus and determination to their future.

2. Know your mental and emotional strengths and weaknesses.

So much of a game relies on mental and emotional strengths. When you know the game mentally, know what you need to do, can anticipate plays and get in the flow, then you're on your way to succeeding.

Those chances of success are enhanced by your ability to use your emotions to your advantage, to use your drive and desire to fuel your play while keeping negative emotions in check. If you know you are vulnerable to taunting from opponents, don't get into word games with them, just focus on your own game. If you know you get overexcited in tense moments, and this adversely affects your game, focus on brief mental images or cues to keep you focused and calm.

Assess where you excel mentally and emotionally and look to shore up weaknesses while building on strengths.

3. Visualize success.

Troy Hawkins was talking to the media after he led his high school football team to a stunning upset in the state play–offs. The only one that wasn't surprised by the upset was Troy. "I never doubted that we'd win," he said. "I knew what we had to do, and before the game I saw us executing the way we needed to win. Then we just went out and did it."

Troy used visualization techniques to improve his perform-ance. Another example: A free–throw shooter in basketball, while preparing to take her shot, sees in her mind's eye her flawless technique and the ball nestling in the net before she shoots. This visualization helps her muscle memory respond in the way she has learned to shoot and gives her confidence that she can execute proper shooting technique.

No matter your sport, you can visualize successful technique before the game and during lulls in the· action (e.g., in the on-deck circle in baseball, in the huddle in football, in between serves in tennis, during a time-out in any sport). Fill your thoughts with visions of success, of you properly executing techniques and tactics, of you achieving your goals. Keep these thoughts of success with you at all times. When you think about your sport, you should be seeing yourself performing successfully in it.

4. Build mental stamina.

Seasons are long and require not only physical endurance but mental stamina as well. Stamina is especially required in dry spells when nothing seems to be going right. Mental stamina comes into play in individual games as well: in a tight contest, the stress wears players down mentally as well as physically. A lot of times you see close games decided on mental errors—an unforced turnover, a botched play, time-outs called when the team has no time-outs left. Players who commit these errors are mentally running on empty, and their actions reflect that.

You can build mental stamina by focusing only on the moment and not on what is riding on that moment. Don't reflect on a past mistake or missed opportunity, don't ponder what's going to happen in the next minute; focus on the here and now and on proper execution. Keep locked in. Players who can do that have the mental stamina it takes to play well when they're tired or the game's on the line.

5. Control emotional swings.

Sarah's softball team had just suffered a tough extra-inning loss to a team they should have beaten. The loss put them in a hole that was going to be tough to dig out of as they battled to win their conference. Sarah herself had not had a particularly good game; her late-inning error allowed the other team to tie the score. After the game, her teammates were moping. Some were dejected and depressed, others were upset or angry.

"Come on!" Sarah told her teammates. "It's one game. We've got to put it behind us and focus on our next game."

She's right. Just as a season is long, and even individual games can be quite wearing on players mentally and physically, seasons and games also have their emotional ups and downs. The players who can control their personal emotional swings are the ones who are poised to succeed, because they don't fall prey to riding the emotional roller coaster that comes with participating in sports.

When you are in control of your emotions, you are also more likely to be in control of your physical abilities. When you're upset or angry or frustrated, your focus is off and you are less likely to execute as well as you can. Remain in emotional control by keeping the big picture in mind. Use visualization to help you maintain control and keep focused on proper execution of skills and tactics.

6. Let go of mistakes, losses, anger, fear.
When you dwell on mistakes, you are prone to make more mistakes. When you let anger or fear take over, your play is adversely affected. When you pout over a tough loss, you aren't fully focused on preparing for the next game.

To be mentally tough, you have to let mistakes, losses, anger, and fear wash off you like water off a duck's back. Don't let it stick to you, because it becomes baggage you have to haul around and slows down your game. The best players are those who can let these things go in the heat of battle—and then turn around and make a big play, ignoring whatever negative emotions they might have been tempted to give in to.

Again, focus on the positive, visualize successful execution, and keep your cool no matter the situation. When games heat up, it's the cool heads that prevail.

Greg Norman: Moving Toward His Next Victory

Greg Norman has enjoyed phenomenal success as a golfer: he has twenty PGA Tour victories, about sixty other victories, he has won the British Open twice, he owns fifty-six international titles, he was elected to World Golf's Hall of Fame in 2001, and he was the first PGA Tour player to surpass $10 million in career earnings. The success has not sapped him of his drive to improve his game. Norman has bounced back from tough defeats, including heartbreaking losses at major championships, with renewed determination, confidence, and focus.

He has used that same approach to succeed off the links as well. He has numerous business ventures under the umbrella of his Great White Shark Enterprises, Inc., including his own golf course design company, production company, an e-commerce company, an athletic turf company, an investments company, a winery, and a restaurant.

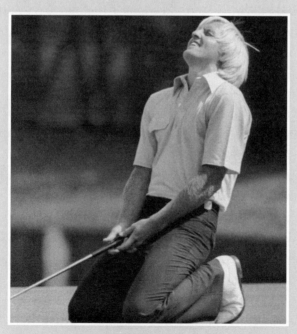

Greg Norman—finding success on the links and in numerous business ventures.

7. Play sharp, stay focused.

Terry was a good tennis player who often easily defeated his opponent. But in tight matches he had the habit of mentally drifting as the match progressed. His mental drifting led to physical mistakes and he lost a lot of matches that he should have won. For some reason, he wasn't able to remain focused.

When you are mentally tough, you are aiding yourself in the battle to play sharp and remain focused. Fans marvel about how some players seem to always come through in the clutch; after a game, the player who came through shrugs his shoulders and says, "The shot was there and I hit it, that's all." Or, "I got my pitch and just focused on hitting a line drive somewhere." Or, "I got open, got the pass, and kicked the goal."

All easy in one sense—just the simple execution of skills—but all so difficult when the game is close and time is winding down, and when physical and mental energies might be low. It's the players who can stay sharp and focused, keep mentally in the game and still be a step ahead, anticipating plays and knowing how to respond, who give those postgame interviews telling how they won the game.

8. Be prepared to play.

Mental toughness helps you prepare to play no matter the situation, whether you're on your own court or field against a weak opponent, or on the road against a strong opponent. Whether you're in the play-offs with your backs against the wall, or entering a hostile environment where you know boos are going to be rained down upon you, you have to be prepared to play. And that calls on a strong dose of mental toughness, on keeping your focus and your cool, on using your adrenaline and your emotions and your mental abilities to your advantage.

That also means not letting bad calls affect your play—or letting anything else affect it. Remind yourself that the field or court is the same no matter where you play, the rules are the same, your purpose is the same. Focus on your team's game plan and your part in executing it. That's all your coach wants you to do and it's all you *can* do. You can't change how a crowd responds or what an official calls. You can control how you play—and when you come prepared to play, you are likely to maximize your performance regardless of the circumstances.

Mental toughness transforms good athletes into great ones, and great ones into legends. Don't overlook mental abilities in your quest to be the best player you can be.

BE THE ULTIMATE TEAM PLAYER

I've talked about the prima donnas who have talent but do more damage than good to a team. I've also talked about players who have the physical talent but who either don't work hard enough in the off-season or during the season to accomplish what they could, or who don't have the mental skills to complement their physical abilities. These players fall in the "could have, should have" category, and their unfulfilled promise proves a constant frustration to their coaches, teammates, fans, and themselves.

To put it all together you have to have the physical skills, the mental abilities and toughness, the attitude, the work ethic, and many other traits and characteristics that I covered in Chapter 1. Rather than repeat those traits, I'm going to add three items to that list. To be the ultimate team player, you have to also

- be able to communicate well with coaches, teammates, and the media
- respect yourself, others, and the game
- know how to add value to your game

Be Able to Communicate Well with Coaches, Teammates, Media

Let's say you're a soccer player and you've just had the ball stolen from you. Your coach pulls you from the game as soon as possible and screams at you on the sidelines, "How many times have I told you to get rid of the ball before you're trapped? Johnson was wide open for a pass!"

The coach is frustrated because, to him, you don't appear to be listening to instructions he has been giving you. Deep down, the coach wants to help you improve your technique and your ability to see the whole field, but chances are good that his message on the sidelines is going to be lost on you, because all you really hear is you're a lousy player.

Communication skills are vital in sports. You have to be on the same page as your coach and teammates. You have to be able to send and receive messages both verbally and nonverbally. Nonverbal communication—facial expressions, body language—is especially important, because it represents more than 70 percent of what we communicate to others.

Think about what you communicate to your coach without having to say a word in the huddle or in practice: you might look glum, or disinterested, or despondent. Or maybe you look eager, attentive, tuned in. Or perhaps you look frustrated, angry, or sullen. Or you might look fearful or tentative. Each look communicates a clear message without you saying a word.

Communication in sports can be difficult because the experience is packed with emotion. It can be hard to be in control of our emotions in pressure-packed moments. The emotional nature of sports is just one of the challenges that athletes face in communicating well with coaches and teammates. Other challenges include:

- You say the right thing but at the wrong time. For example, you don't wait until a critical moment in a ball game to tell your coach you don't understand the play she's sending in, and your coach shouldn't overload you with detailed, technical instruction in the middle of a game. That should be saved for the next practice.

- The person who is communicating lacks the verbal or nonverbal skills to send the message. This causes the message to be misunderstood.

- The message isn't received because the person it's intended for isn't really listening—that is, the person thinks he already *knows* what you're going to say and he's just preparing his rebuttal as you speak.

- The message is received but it's misinterpreted, as in the case of the soccer coach yelling at his player because the player didn't pass the ball at the right time.

- Communication breaks down because you feel the other person doesn't care what you think, doesn't want to hear your message. So eventually you stop communicating with that person.

So what do you need to do as a player to communicate better? You need to work on your listening skills. You need to be in control of your emotions as you communicate. You need to think about what your message is and how you deliver it. You need to think about your body language and what it expresses. You need to try to break down any walls, if there are any, between you and your coach or any teammates. You need to talk to your coach, away from practice, if you have a problem or concern about how she is communicating with you and how she might be interpreting your messages.

Don't let problems with coaches or teammates fester. Ignoring a problem only makes it worse, and in sports it can disrupt a team, upset the delicate balance between harmony and discord, and derail an otherwise good team. Communicate your feelings and concerns with respect and with patience. Don't expect your coach or teammates to know how you feel just because it seems evident to you. Clue them in appropriately—and then be ready to listen to their concerns and feelings as well.

Alex Rodriguez: Getting His Message Across

When Alex Rodriguez signed a ten-year, $252 million deal with the Texas Rangers in the winter of 2000, he took a lot of heat from the media and fans for signing such a large deal. How did he respond? By letting his bat and glove do his talking for him. They spoke loudly and clearly, as A-Rod had his best season ever in 2001 (52 home runs, 135 runs batted in). In the spring of 2004, in a deal that rocked the sports world, he joined the Yankees, the most storied franchise in baseball history.

The perennial All-Star, who has the major-league single-season record for home runs by a shortstop (57, in 2002) and who is the youngest player ever to hit 300 home runs, is happy to share his wealth and his time, especially with young kids. In 1998, he founded the Alex Rodriguez Foundation, which works extensively with the Boys & Girls Clubs of Miami, where he grew up. He also indirectly helps Boys & Girls Clubs across the nation, as Microsoft provides over $1,000 in software to local Boys & Girls Clubs every time Rodriguez drives in a run. Rodriguez is a national spokesperson for Boys & Girls Clubs of America.

Two other notes about communication: sometimes teams really click because they communicate well on the court or field. A hand gesture here, a nod there, a certain look or a well-placed word at the right time often results in your team gaining an advantage. The better you know your teammates, and the better you are at communicating effectively with them during games, the better your team will be. And the more fun the game will be.

Said another way, when you're on the same page as your coach and your teammates, the experience is more fun.

Finally, you might have occasion to be interviewed by the media. Your words will be aired over the radio or printed in the newspaper. You might be interviewed on local TV. What you say and how you say it will communicate a lot to the public—about you (and by inference about how you have been raised), about your coach, about your team, about your school. A lot of people will be interpreting the message you send.

Be respectful of the interviewer and of the situation—and know you don't have to spill your guts or divulge your deepest thoughts about the issue. Keep your demeanor upbeat and positive (I'm not saying to not be yourself, but do present a positive image). You can put some emotion into your message, but be careful that it's not at the expense of others—that your message doesn't put down other players or your coach or your opponents or the game officials.

Enjoy your time with the media. Just monitor yourself to make sure that you don't say something you later regret.

Communication is a two-way street. If you expect to be heard, be prepared to listen. It's amazing how many messages are misinterpreted because the receiver isn't really listening.

Respect Yourself, Others, and the Game

Respect is one of the keys to good communication, and it's central to the way you comport yourself as an athlete. It's really quite simple: when you respect yourself, you are going to get more out of your talent. Why? Because by respecting yourself, that means you appreciate your talents, you take them seriously, you take who you are seriously, and you behave in a manner that tells other people that they should take you seriously. You command respect from others when you respect yourself.

Notice I said *command*, not *demand*. The respect from others comes automatically when they see that you take yourself seriously. Respect has nothing to do with ego or big proclamations about how good you are. In fact, self-respect can be quiet and calm, but its presence is very evident. People are drawn to those who have self-respect, because, deep down, they want to have that same self–respect—and they know they are likely to be appreciated by that person.

When you have self–respect, you typically respect other people as well—your coach, your teammates, game officials, your opponents. When you respect others, that means you appreciate who they are and what they can do and what they say. That means you listen to your coach and teammates and when problems arise you talk them out. That means you see the skills your teammates have and you look to help them utilize those skills more. That means you respect their feelings and opinions even when they differ from yours.

That also means you don't argue calls with officials or get into trash–talking debates with opponents. There are ways that you can respectfully talk to an official. You can ask for an interpretation of a call in a way that doesn't disrespect the official. (Many leagues allow only team captains to talk to officials, so make sure you know your league rules.)

Finally, respect the game. That's really the flip side of the coin of respecting yourself. When you respect the game, you're more likely to respect yourself, and vice versa. Respecting the game means giving it your all—not only in games but in practices and in your off-season preparation. It means learning as much as you can about the game, the requisite skills and tactics, and the game's history. It means respecting not only the letter of the law—the rules—but the spirit behind the rules. It means being a good sport. It means appreciating your time in the sun, because that time doesn't last forever.

Pelé: Earning Respect for Himself, His Country, and the Game of Soccer

Perhaps you have not heard of Edson Arantes do Nascimento. But people all over the world are familiar with the name he is commonly known by, the name synonymous with soccer and Brazil and excellence: Pelé. *O Rei* is another title given to him by his fans, and it means "The King." In Brazil, he is more than

Pelé, the King of Soccer, commanded respect both on and off the field. He was named the No. 1 Athlete of the Century by the world's National Olympic Committees (NOC), even though he never played in an Olympic game. He topped Muhammed Ali, Michael Jordan, Carl Lewis, and Mark Spitz. Pelé was named Athlete of the Century by eight other international organizations in addition to the NOC.

a champion athlete; he is a national hero and a global ambassador. They call him *Perola Negra*—the Black Pearl. Before David Beckham, before the soccer mom phenomenon took hold in the United States, Pelé brought the sport of *futebol* to the world stage, even though a form of this game had been played for centuries.

Pelé earned great respect throughout his career, not only because of his talent as a player, but also because he respected others and he never forgot his roots. He was born to a very poor family on October 23, 1940, in Tres Coracoes in Brazil. As a child he lived in the city of Bauru, shined shoes for pennies, learned soccer from his father, and played for a local minor league team. At age eleven, Pelé was discovered by Waldemar de Brito, one of Brazil's best former players. Brito was able to convince Pelé to move to Santos to play for the national team at age fifteen. Within two years, Pelé led them to a World Cup victory—and he repeated this feat in 1962 and 1970.

Upon Pelé's retirement in 1974, J. B. Pinheiro, Brazil's ambassador to the U.N., said Pelé had "spent twenty-two years playing soccer, and in that time he has done more for goodwill and friendship than all of the ambassadors ever appointed." Pelé said that being a goodwill ambassador for Brazil—and for soccer itself—was of primary importance to him.

He was exceptionally adept at using his platform as a sports legend to communicate his optimism for mankind. "The most important thing I have learned is that essentially sport is the best medium through which we can communicate. I saw the world because of soccer and got to know things and, more important, I got to know people," he says in his 1976 book, *Play Football with Pelé*. "All these people that I have met have made me have faith in the future of mankind. I believe that one day we will be able to unite in a team, a greater team called humanity."

After retiring for one year, he signed a three-year contract with the New York Cosmos of the now-defunct North American Soccer League (NASL). He became the highest paid athlete in the world, but said his motive was to popularize the game in the United States. During the pregame ceremonies for his final game in the NASL, Pelé appealed to his captive audience of more than 75,000 fans to direct attention and love to the world's children.

A cabinet position was created for him, Minister of Sports, and he used his popularity to attract funding for amateur sports leagues for youth in the impoverished inner cities of Brazil. Pelé also used this position to fight for the right of players to be free agents.

His other off-the-field successes include writing several bestselling autobiographies, starring in several documentary and semidocumentary films, and composing numerous musical pieces, including the entire soundtrack for the film *Pelé* (1977). He was the 1978 recipient of the International Peace Award, received an honorary British knighthood, and was named Goodwill Ambassador by UNICEF.

With all of his accolades and admirers throughout the decades, Pelé has always been confident in his abilities, yet humble about his own role in his success. He gives credit to his dream team in *Play Football with Pelé:* "Are we what people say we are? I sometimes think that I am not the man that people say I am. I am sure of one thing—I am not alone. I owe what I am today to many people. They all, in their different ways, taught me something," he writes. "In life, none of us is alone. We are always part of a team and each one has his own special function. Every individual is important. . . . I only became what I am today because I was helped, encouraged, advised, taught, stimulated and criticized."

Career Highlights
1,282 goals in 1,363 matches
Scored an average of one goal in every international game he played
Top Brazilian goalscorer of all time
Named Athlete of the Century by nine worldwide organizations

Club Titles
1957 Top goalscorer in Sao Paulo league (17 goals)
1958 Top goalscorer in Sao Paulo league (58 goals)
1959 Copa America finalist
1959 Top goalscorer in Sao Paulo league (45 goals)
1960 Top goalscorer in Sao Paulo league (33 goals)
1961 Top goalscorer in Sao Paulo league (47 goals)

1961 Copa Libertadores (Santos)

1961 Brazilian Cup winner (Santos)

1962 Top goalscorer in Sao Paulo league (37 goals)

1962 Copa Libertadores (Santos)

1962 World Club champion (Santos)

1962 Brazilian Cup winner (Santos)

1963 Top goalscorer in Sao Paulo league (22 goals)

1963 World Club champion (Santos)

1963 Brazilian Cup winner (Santos)

1964 Top goalscorer in Sao Paulo league (34 goals)

1964 Brazilian Cup winner (Santos)

1965 Top goalscorer in Sao Paulo league (49 goals)

1965 Brazilian Cup winner (Santos)

1968 Brazilian Cup winner (Santos)

1969 Top goalscorer in Sao Paulo league (26 goals)

1973 Top goalscorer in Sao Paulo league (11 goals)

1977 USA champion (Cosmos New York)

International Honors

World Cup (1958, '62, '70)

World Club Championship (1962, '63)

Sao Paulo State Championship (1956, '58, '60, '61, '62, '64, '65, '67, '68)

1958 FIFA World Cup in Sweden: winner

1959 Copa America: finalist

1959 Top goalscorer in Copa America (9 goals)

1962 FIFA World Cup in Chile: winner

1966 FIFA World Cup in England: first round

1970 FIFA World Cup in Mexico: winner

92 caps, 97 goals

Know How to Add Value to Your Game

To improve your athletic performance and become as complete a player as you can, you need to: diligently train in the off-season;

continually hone your physical and mental skills; learn how to be an effective communicator; and respect yourself, others connected with the game, and the game itself. All of these add value to your game.

Another way you add value to your game is to see the game and the team through your coach's eyes: What does your coach need you to do? In what ways can you help your team the most? What skills do you need to learn or improve? Is your attitude in the right place? Are you in good condition? Do you understand the strategies and tactics of your sport well enough that you can *make* things happen out there rather than reacting to things *after* they happen?

Coaches love players who are extensions of themselves on the court or field—that is, they play the game as the coach sees it. These players know the game backward and forward, know the nuances of the flow, know when to attack and when to retreat, know the type of defense or offense that will best work against a particular opponent, know when to call a time-out to stop the flow. They know what's called for without the coach telling them.

To get to this point takes years of firsthand experience as well as learning from watching how the best collegiate and professional players approach the game. When you're serious about the game and respect it well enough to learn as much as you can about it, then you're on the road to adding value to your game.

> If you want to add immediate value to your game, focus on your team's needs rather than your own. Become a selfless player. This doesn't mean passing up shots or opportunities—it means taking them at the right times, and at all times making the best decisions that will help your team.

We covered a lot of ground in this chapter in considering how you can improve your athletic performance. But it's really up to you; you have to make the right choices and put in the effort. The last chapter is all about you and the choices you make.

Magic Johnson was a huge star on the court and an even bigger success off it.

8

IT ALL DEPENDS ON YOU

MAGIC JOHNSON: BUILDING AN EMPIRE

Nothing can slow Magic Johnson down. Not Larry Bird, when Magic's Michigan State team knocked off Bird's Indiana State team in the 1979 NCAA basketball championship game. Not an injury to teammate Kareem Abdul-Jabbar in Game 6 of the 1980 NBA championship against Philadelphia; Magic, who normally played guard, filled in at center in Game 7 and led the Los Angeles Lakers to victory with 42 points, 15 rebounds, 7 assists, and 3 steals.

Not a knee injury the following year; Magic returned the next year to lead the league in steals and to lead the Lakers to another NBA title, in which he was named Most Valuable Player.

Not even Magic's most formidable foe, HIV, which he announced in 1991 that he had tested positive for. He retired from the NBA, though he came back to play in the All-Star game—and led the West to victory while earning MVP honors. His performance in that game typified what he did throughout his career (see the box below).

Magic Johnson NBA Highlights

Career: Thirteen years, all with the Los Angeles Lakers
Member of five NBA championship teams
NBA Regular Season MVP three times
NBA Championship Finals MVP three times

Twelve-time All-Star

Nine-time member of All-NBA First Team

Elected to the NBA's 50th Anniversary All-Time Team and to the Hall of Fame

Points: 17,707 (19.5 per game)

Rebounds: 6,559 (7.2 per game)

Assists: 10,141 (11.2 per game)

Steals: 1,724 (ninth on the all-time list)

Four years later, Magic made a comeback midway through the season. He played well, led the Lakers to the play–offs once again, and retired for good after that.

Magic might have retired, but he is busier than ever. He is a vice president of the Lakers. He runs an empire of Magic Johnson Theaters, Starbucks coffeehouses, and restaurants (T.G.I. Friday's and Fatburger restaurants). His Johnson Development Corporation serves to foster economic growth in minority urban and suburban neigh–borhoods. The Magic Johnson Foundation, founded in 1991, focuses on improving and addressing the health, educational, and social needs of people living in the inner city. It also raises awareness about health and social concerns that threaten underserved communities. The Foundation has raised more than $20 million for charity.

An example of the Foundation's work is its partnership with Hewlett–Packard to bridge the "digital divide" in inner cities by opening eight Inventor Centers. The Centers offer technology train–ing and skills development and access to computer online services for underprivileged youths and adults.

Twelve years after announcing he had the AIDS virus, Magic Johnson was supposed to be dead. Instead, he is in the NBA Hall of Fame, his businesses are worth more than $500 million, and he is giving back to communities, to urban areas, to underprivileged kids. He wants to give children the tools they need to succeed, and he firmly believes that if they are given those tools, they will have a positive future.

Magic himself has always been positive about his future. "The medicine has done its thing," he told *USA Today*. "And God has done His part. It's mind over matter, too. I've never felt I would be sick or get sick. I thought I would be here."

IT'S YOUR CHOICE

Magic Johnson decided he wanted to excel at the highest levels in sports and out of sports, and he has let nothing get in his way. It's up to you how much you want to excel in sports and in life. No one can do it for you. You can learn all the principles of success that there are, but you have to decide whether you want to apply them.

Don't read into that that I think your road to success is easy. It's not. It's a long road, filled with twists and turns, with trials and setbacks, with dangers and disappointments. But you can traverse that road. You can make as much of your life as you dare to make of it. You can get the most out of your abilities and apply those abilities in ways you perhaps never dreamed of until recently, both in sports and beyond.

You can do that by following the principles that I outlined in this book. The Move Without the Ball program, which is part workbook, part planner, and wholly interactive, can help you put those principles into action.

I'm not promising you riches and fame. I'm promising you that if you faithfully follow the principles I've laid out in this book, you'll be moving toward the great potential that you have. You might not have even considered your potential beyond sports yet, but I can guarantee you that it's there. And if you haven't considered it yet, you're at an exciting time in your life, because you are just beginning on a great journey.

Just don't shortchange yourself and see it solely as a *sports* journey. If you take any message with you from this book, I hope that it's this: Yes, sports are part of life and bring many good things, and you should pursue your dreams there. But you should not pursue those sports dreams at the expense of your other dreams—and if you don't have other dreams, start dreaming. Apply what you have learned from your sports endeavors to help you succeed in other areas of your life. Broaden your horizons. In sports you tend to succeed when you attack, as opposed to sitting back and reacting to your opponent's attack. It's the "trying to win" approach versus the "trying not to lose" approach—when you're "trying not to lose," you're tentative, back on your heels, your actions dictated by your opponent's actions; you're just trying to hold on.

It's the same in life: Don't sit back, tentative and fearful, just trying to hold on and reacting to whatever it brings you. Attack life with a hunger, a confidence, and a plan that focuses on your strengths and talents. Stop thinking small. If you think that sports are your only way out, your only avenue to success, think again—and in much bigger terms. Sports are one small part of life, and an athletic career is very unlikely for 99.99 percent of high school players. That's a pretty big percent of players who are going to be making livings in ways *other* than playing sports.

Your eyes should be opened now to the wide variety of choices and opportunities that you have beyond sports. It's up to you to decide on how you want to pursue success in your life, how you plan to reach your potential, how you want to focus your education and eventually forge a career path for yourself.

The choice is yours. Are you ready to make it?

Wayne Gretzky: Not Afraid to Take His Shots

Wayne Gretzky set sixty-one National Hockey League (NHL) scoring records in his twenty seasons. He was a ten-time scoring champion and won the Most Valuable Player award nine times. He led the Edmonton Oilers to four Stanley Cup titles. He is the all-time NHL leader in points (2,857), goals (894), and assists (1,963). He is also the all-time NHL leader in those categories in the play-offs.

It was Gretzky who coined the phrase "You'll always miss

100 percent of the shots you don't take." Now head of operations and managing partner of the NHL's Phoenix Coyotes, and owner of his own restaurant in Toronto, Gretzky teaches his kids that life and sports are very similar—and that passion can make up for a lack of talent.

Wayne Gretzky—passionate about hockey and about life.

MAKE SUCCESS A HABIT

Habits are hard to make and hard to break. We tend to make habits when we are rewarded in some way for those habits. Thus, many athletes make a habit of working hard in practice, because they know the reward is better performance, and they value that. And there's nothing wrong with that.

As you begin to consider the bigger picture for your life, though, hopefully you will value things beyond sports performance. Doing so will help you form good habits that affect your life beyond sports.

The kernel of success is found in habits. If you make studying a habit, your grades will benefit. If you make training and conditioning a habit, your athletic performance will improve. If you apply yourself to whatever discipline in whatever field you choose, you will continue to uncover new layers of potential within you.

It's all about the daily choices you make—to study, to practice, to apply your talents, to focus on the positive, to investigate your interests, to plan for your future, to set and move toward goals that can include sports but that go beyond as well.

It's easy to fall into bad habits without even knowing it, habits that can negatively impact your future. A few examples are sliding by in school because sports are the only thing that interests you; getting involved in drinking, drugs, or other illicit behavior; working halfheartedly at an after-school or summer job because it's "only" a minimum-wage job. These approaches to life carry over and affect you both now and later on. If you do poorly in school, your college choices are limited and you have to struggle to open up those choices again. If you drink or do drugs, you greatly limit your opportunities, and you increase your risk of getting in trouble with the law and of permanently damaging your health and life.

Yet those choices are just as easy to develop into habits as are the more positive choices that I previously mentioned. The choices really are yours, and they really do matter.

Be wise in them. Respect yourself—your body, your mind, your abilities, your potential—and respect others around you. Do the lit-tle things right day in and day out, and you'll find that, without even knowing it, you are making success a habit.

Yao Ming: Carving Out His Own Success

You might remember Yao Ming in the commercial for Visa, where he asks a clerk if he can write a check. "Yo!" the clerk responds sarcastically, pointing to a sign behind her that says "Absolutely no checks." Yao thinks the clerk is trying to say his name, and he politely says, "Yao." The exchange continues in confusing and humorous fashion.

That's the second commercial Yao has done since joining the NBA in 2002—witness that the very tall (seven-feet-five) player from China will do quite well on his own here in the United States. Both his parents played on the Chinese National Team, but Yao has already surpassed their basketball success and is carving out his own niche—not only on the court but in the media as well.

KEEP ON MOVING

Use the Success Circles that I talked about in Chapter 4 to keep moving toward success. Plan for your continual growth in personal and career development, health and fitness, and athletic perform-ance. Return often to those circles, update them, revise them, keep them going, keep expanding, keep moving.

Remember the keys to moving without the ball, which I pre-sented in Chapter 2:

- **Expand your vision beyond sports.** Take what you've learned from any success you've achieved in sports and apply it elsewhere.

- **Know your passions and abilities.** Don't focus on "being successful" in general, with success being your desired outcome; focus on using your abilities to follow your passions beyond sports. Success will come as a result of this focus.

- **Check your attitude.** If you're doubtful or negative, if you're tentative or angry at the world or defensive, you're handicapping yourself in your personal pursuits. Focus on your strengths, on your positives, and look to make your own breaks. Be resilient and bounce back from defeats. Have an attitude that is cheerfully and steadfastly defiant in the face of challenges and setbacks, one that says "I will overcome."

- **Set and move toward goals.** Use goals to help you plan your course of action and to measure how you're doing along the way. Incorporate these goals into your Success Circles.

- **Learn from others.** You're not in this alone. Gain support, encouragement, wisdom, and guidance from an array of people. Hook up with a mentor, especially one in a field of your interest, if possible. Gain insight from both adults and peers, and apply that insight to your own life.

- **Make a game plan.** Don't just *let* things happen in your life; *make* them happen. Plan for good things to happen, and plot out how to take the steps to make them happen. Be flexible in your plans; just as you revise your Success Circles along the way, you should revise your game plan as well (in fact, your Success Circles can act as your game plan spelled out). The point is to have a plan that uses your strengths and talents and steers you toward fulfilling your dreams.

- **Make the daily choice.** I talked about this a few moments ago. The choices are in front of you on a daily basis. When you consistently make good choices, good things are going to happen in your life.

Remember to believe in yourself, to challenge yourself, to make learning a lifelong experience, to think outside the box, to be flexible and adaptable, to keep things in perspective, to keep growing and moving throughout your life.

By all means, move *with* the ball while you can. Move with it to the best of your ability and enjoy every minute of it—even the gut-wrenching practices and the monotony and boredom of diligent off-season training. Enjoy the adrenaline rush of playing before crowds, of playing in tight ball games, of performing at your best, of winning games, of exceeding your own expectations and those of your coach. Enjoy the bus rides to away games, the camaraderie with your team-mates, the jokes, the fun, the bonding that takes place when you are part of a group that is working hard and putting lots of "sweat equity" into achieving its goals. Enjoy the pure exhaustion you feel at the end of a hard game or practice, the cold sweetness of water as you slake your thirst after sweating out several pounds, the high fives for a play well done or a game well played. Enjoy the knowl-edge that you gave it all you had, you poured everything into your preparation and your playing, you left it all out on the court or field or mat or track. Enjoy even the lessons you learn from bitter defeat, one of them being that life *does* go on and you *can* bounce back.

Enjoy all this and everything else that your status as an athlete brings you.

And at the same time begin to move *without* the ball. Because as you do, you will find enjoyment in that that will not fade away, that will not diminish to sweet memory over time. Your greatest moments in sports are nearing an end, even if that end is yet several years away—but your greatest moments in life, when you learn how to move without the ball, are fast approaching.

AFTERWORD

Now that you've finished *Move Without the Ball*, you should understand the need for having a plan in mind for your life that goes
beyond sports. And you should know the keys to excelling in both
sports and in life, to overcoming challenges and building life skills
that can serve you no matter what career path you choose, and to
being healthy and fit.

However, *knowing* something and putting it into *action* are sometimes two separate things. So, with the help of some top-level educators in South Carolina, I developed a Move Without the Ball program
to assist you in gaining a greater vision for your life and in creating
the game plan to move toward that vision.

The program is based on my Nine Steps Success Process, which is
detailed in my book *Teens Can Make It Happen*. Through this process,
you will be able to put into action what you've learned in *Move
Without the Ball*. The program includes a Move Without the Ball student workbook that gives you an overview of each of the Nine Steps
and provides activities and exercises that help you set and achieve
your goals in sports and beyond.

This program was created with the help, as I said, of some great
educators, under the leadership of Dr. Ronald Carter, provost and
dean of the faculty at Coker College in Hartsville, South Carolina.
Besides Ron, a longtime friend of mine, those involved in develop-

ing the Move Without the Ball program were these South Carolina educators:

Coker College
- Dr. B. James Dawson, president
- Dr. James W. Lemke, director of the Center for Research, Leadership, and Community Development
- Dr. James Holbrook, associate professor of physical education and sports studies, Coker College

Darlington Schools
- Pearl Jeffords, principal, Darlington Junior High School
- James Peterson, assistant principal, Darlington High School
- Willie Shaw, guidance counselor, Darlington High School
- Sharon Moon, child nutrition supervisor, Darlington County School District

Hartsville High School
- Chris Alexander, coordinating teacher, Hartsville High School
- Candace Holcomb, assistant principal, Hartsville High School

Sonovista Alternative School
- Col. Walter Carpenter, ROTC
- Sgt. James Nelson, ROTC

Byerly Foundation
- Dick Puffer, executive director, Byerly Foundation

Communities in Schools
- Dorothy Richardson, chair of the board, Communities in Schools

Hartsville YES! Planning Committee
- Tim Griggs, director of athletics and associate professor of physical education, Coker College

- Katie Paté, women's intercollegiate basketball coach and senior women's administrator, Coker College
- Ernie James, director of human resources, Coker College
- Larry Reiss, marketing teacher, Coker College
- Terry Small, president of Advanced Medical, LLC
- Dr. Stephen B. Terry, vice president for student and enrollment services, Coker College

I'd also like to thank Wendy Graham, who directed the development of the Move Without the Ball program, and Tom Hanlon, who helped write the resources for the program.

The combined efforts of all of these people have resulted in a dynamic, practical, real-world program that will help you achieve your best, in sports and out.

GRATEFUL ACKNOWLEDGMENT TO THE FOLLOWING SOURCES:

Corbis for photographs of Vince Carter, Dikembe Mutombo, Charles Barkley, Paul Wylie, Walter Payton, Mia Hamm, Peter Ueberroth, Ulice Payne Jr., Bo Jackson, Hank Aaron, Darryl Strawberry, Franco Harris, Julius Erving, Cal Ripken, Kevin Johnson, Serena Williams, Pam Shriver, Bryon Russell, Jerry Rice, Barry Bonds, Lynn Swann, Lyle Alzado, Dave Winfield, Greg Norman, Magic Johnson, Wayne Gretzky, Pelé, and Gertrude Ederle.

The *Chicago Sun-Times* for photograph of Yarmo Green.

ABOUT THE AUTHOR

Stedman Graham is chairman and CEO of S. Graham & Associates (SGA), a management and marketing consulting company that creates customized training and leadership development programs for corporate and educational markets.

As a sought-out speaker and lecturer, he presents to corporations, organizations, and nonprofits. Clients include Merrill Lynch, Wells Fargo, Georgia Pacific, National Intramural-Recreational Sports Association, American College of Sports Medicine, YMCA, Hyatt Hotels Corporation, Manpower, CNN, GlaxoSmithKline, Plains Capital Corporation, U.S. Department of Labor's Job Corps, Harvard and Wharton business schools, U.S. Department of Education, and the U.S. Olympic Committee.

Graham has authored a number of books. His books include two *New York Times* bestsellers, *You Can Make It Happen: A Nine-Step Plan for Success* and *Teens Can Make It Happen: Nine Steps to Success; You Can Make It Happen Every Day*, a motivational pocketbook; *Build Your Own Life Brand!*, which explores the concept of personal branding; and *The Ultimate Guide to Sports Marketing*, an industry textbook which he coauthored. Graham's most recent book, *Move Without the Ball*, is a collection of principles and teachings for student athletes and nonathletes that encourages them to widen their definition of a successful life and increase their career options by building a solid academic foundation.

Actively involved in education, he is an adjunct professor at the University of Chicago and the University of Illinois at Chicago where he teaches a leadership course based on his Nine-Step Process. At the Kellogg Graduate School of Management at Northwestern University, he taught a management strategy course titled "The Dynamics of

Leadership." He founded and directed George Washington University's Forum for Sport and Event Management and Marketing—the first of its kind in the country.

Graham has shown a lifelong commitment to youth and community. In 1985, Graham founded AAD (Athletes Against Drugs) Education, Health and Sports, a nonprofit organization of athletes and other civic leaders committed to developing leadership in underserved youths. An organization with over 500 professional athletes, AAD has served over 15,000 students and has awarded $1.5 million in scholarships. Graham serves on several boards, including the national board of Junior Achievement (JA) and the 7-Eleven Education Is Freedom Foundation, and he is a member of the Economic Club of Chicago.

Graham holds a bachelor's degree in social work from Hardin-Simmons University. He received a master's degree in education from Ball State University and an honorary doctorate in humanities from Coker College, where he is also a distinguished visiting professor.